THE MAKING OF DOCTOR WHO

PRIMETIME

Creating a Monster

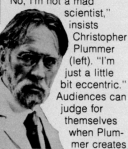

"No, I'm not a mad scientist," insists Christopher Plummer (left). "I'm just a little bit eccentric." Audiences can judge for themselves when Plummer creates a walking, talking robot (played by *St. Elsewhere*'s David Morse) in "Prototype," a future two-hour CBS TV-movie. In the film, Plummer plays a Nobel Prize-winner who lets loose his ultimate creation upon an unsuspecting world. But, claims the actor, "It's just a charming story about the relationship between a visionary and his experiment." Isn't that what Frankenstein said?

Identity Crisis

What's in a name? A lawsuit, maybe. That's what Columbia Pictures Television decided while mounting its summer adaptation of the BBC series *The Fall and Rise of Reginald Perrin*, scheduled to premiere on ABC Aug. 2. The show is now called *Reggie*—and the surname of the lead character has been changed to Potter. "They thought Perrin sounded too British," says series star Richard (*Soap*) Mulligan (above). And, perhaps, too litigious. The show is set in Little Neck, Long Island, where Columbia's legal department uncovered a real-life Reginald Perrin, thus necessitating the surname switch.

Happy Birthday to *Who*?

U.S. fans of the British science-fiction series *Doctor Who* may be justifiably confused next November. Lionheart Television, the U.S. syndicator, has come up with the gimmick of staging a 20th birthday celebration for the show—and aims to get some seven million fans to sing "Happy Birthday" to the good Doctor. But to Whom? Five actors have played Doctor Who—and three, Tom Baker (below left), Peter Davison (right) and Jon Pertwee, still appear over here.

20

INSIDER

Joke, Am I? Choke on *This*, Fool!

Here's sports columnist Dick Young, writing in The Sporting News, on *The A-Team*'s Mr. T (right): "When Mr. T was around the boxing beat as bodyguard to Leon Spinks, standing in gyms in a tuxedo, with earrings

Gene Trindl

and that absurd Mohican [actually Mandinkan] hair-do, looking fierce and never saying boo, sports-writers all took him as a joke, a put-on. Now, he's cleaning up as a TV star. Shows you what we know."

Evans: Pounds Away!

It's no surprise that *Dynasty*'s Linda Evans says she has "a terrific metabolism." She admits, though, during a five-part interview on *Good Morning America* the week of July 18, that even she has to diet now and then. Here, in part, is the recipe Evans gives on *GMA* for making her regimen "something you can actually look forward to: Set the table, put out candles, light the fireplace, make [the setting] attractive to yourself. Prepare something you really like, take small portions, take 20 minutes or more to eat it. . . . You're full, you're content, you feel good about yourself and you're happy." And so hungry we need a big bowl of buttered popcorn to get us through *Dynasty*.

Insider's Choice
BRIDESHEAD REVISITED

No kings. No queens. No prime ministers. "It's a little bit different from the period stuff we'd been turning out before," says Anthony Andrews wryly. Indeed, the British mini-series in which Andrews plays the brilliant, unstable Sebastian Flyte is more than just different. In character, pace and acting, this 11-part adaptation of Evelyn Waugh's novel of upper-class anguish is a television classic: worth watching again—and again. *(Brideshead Revisited will be rerun on many PBS stations beginning July 11. Pictured: Jeremy Irons; Andrews; Diana Quick.)*

THE MAKING
OF DOCTOR WHO

*By arrangement with the British Broadcasting
Corporation*

by
TERRANCE DICKS
and
MALCOLM HULKE

A TARGET BOOK
published by
the Paperback Division of
W. H. ALLEN & Co. Ltd.

A Target Book
Published in 1976 in
a Revised and updated edition
by Tandem Publishing Ltd
This edition reprinted in 1980
by the Paperback division of
W. H. Allen & Co. Ltd
A Howard & Wyndham Company
44 Hill St, London, W1X 8LB

Originally published in Great Britain by
Pan Books Ltd, 1972

Printed in Great Britain by
Richard Clay (The Chaucer Press) Ltd, Bungay, Suffolk

ISBN 0 426 11615 1

*Parts of the material in this new edition appeared in 'The Doctor
Who Monster Book' by Terrance Dicks, Target Books 1975*

Contents

THANKS

We wish to thank the following people who have given help with one or both editions of this book:

Philip Hinchcliffe
Robert Holmes
Jack Kine
Barry Letts
Sydney Newman
David Whitaker
Jan Vincent-Rudzki
Stephen Payne

and members of the Doctor Who Appreciation Society

We also wish to thank the many other people, too numerous to be listed, who have helped with advice and information.

Terrance Dicks and Malcolm Hulke

How it all Began

The first episode of the first-ever *Doctor Who* serial was transmitted on Saturday afternoon, 23 November 1963.

Think for a moment what this means. If you were born on that historic Saturday, you will now be at secondary school, unable to remember a time when there wasn't a *Doctor Who*. If you were old enough actually to *watch* it, you could be grown up, married and with children of your own!

About ten million people watch *Doctor Who* every week. With a particularly popular serial those figures zoom even higher. A study by the BBC's Research Unit showed that this huge audience spreads right through the generations. Naturally enough the biggest group of viewers were children in the ten to fifteen age-group. But there was no shortage of younger *and* older viewers —just as many over-fifties as under-fives!

Its incredibly long life, and continuing popularity, make *Doctor Who* one of the most successful shows in British television. How *did* it all begin?

One of the things that makes show-business so exciting—and so nerve-wracking—can be expressed by the well-used phrase—*you never can tell!* No one knows for sure what makes a success. A work written by the most famous of writers, with popular stars in the leading roles, with millions spent on a spectacular production, can finish as a very expensive flop. Luckily the reverse is also true. A modest show on a limited budget, without a single star name, will suddenly take off, and the astonished and delighted producer realises he has a hit on his hands. *Doctor Who*, like many other great men, was born in humble circumstances.

Television is something of an 'instant' medium. Yesterday is already history, last year is lost in the mists of time. So it is no easy matter to reconstruct something that happened over twelve years ago. But here, as accurate as painstaking research can make it, is an account of the origins of *Doctor Who*.

'A crotchety old man in a Police Box'

Even from the beginning, *Doctor Who* was unusual. Most television shows are conceived by an individual writer. He will write a 'format', a few pages of notes on the basic ideas, the characters and possible stories, and send it to a television company. If the company like the idea, they *may* commission a first script. If they like that, they *may* decide to put on the series ...

Doctor Who, however, was created inside the BBC, not by any one person, but by the collaboration of several. This could have been a recipe for disaster. There is an old saying, 'the camel is a horse designed by a committee'. In the case of *Doctor Who*, the committee actually did manage to design a horse—and a thoroughbred champion too!

In 1962, Sydney Newman had recently been appointed Head of Drama at the BBC. One of his senior colleagues was Donald Wilson, then Head of Series and Serials. The two men had much to discuss, and one of the things they talked about was the creation of a new Saturday afternoon serial.

They wanted a show basically for older children, but with something to interest the rest of the family. An adventure serial with a mysterious hero. Some kind of traveller. What about the setting? Historical, present-day—or sometime in the future? *Or why not all three?*

The idea was already beginning to take shape. A traveller through Space *and* Time.

Next step—what should he travel in? Obviously some kind of spaceship. A flying saucer? Expensive to build and difficult to make convincing. Then maybe this space-craft could be so advanced that it had the power to change shape, merge with its surroundings? A nice idea—but they'd have to build a new, disguised space-craft for every serial. But suppose the shape-changing mechanism got stuck? Then the space-craft could always look exactly the same. You could have all the fun of some everyday object appearing in the most incongruous settings. Something simple and familiar—like a Police Box!

This magical Police Box needed a simple but impressive name, possibly something made up from initials. T for Time of course, and S for Space. D for its unique Dimensions—and throw in R for Einstein's Theory of Relativity, for good measure. Time And Relative Dimensions In Space—TARDIS!

Most important of all, what about the hero? Most heroes are young, handsome, charming. 'Let's make him a crotchety old man,' said Sydney Newman, 'and have him about 745 years old!'

Now the basic elements were all there. A mysterious old man, travelling through Space and Time in a space-craft disguised as a Police Box. All he needed was a name. Or did he? Perhaps he shouldn't have a name, just some kind of title. Like ... Doctor. 'Doctor who?' asked someone—and they had their title. *Doctor Who*.

The Doctor needed a motive for his travels. He could be a fugitive, on the run from some unknown danger. Add another complication. The TARDIS already had a faulty change mechanism. Suppose the steering was equally erratic. The Doctor would never arrive exactly when or where he wanted to—a simple way of landing him in the middle of each new adventure.

By now the basic idea was fully evolved. Next step was to hand it over to the people who would be responsible for getting it to the television screen—the Producer and Script Editor.

In television, the Producer has complete and overall charge of his own particular show. Each individual episode, or group of episodes, will have its own Director, responsible for 'getting the show in the can', i.e. for carrying out a successful studio recording. Individual Directors come and go with each serial. The Producer remains with his own show, working with each Director in turn.

This is an enormously demanding and time-consuming job, and in one very important area the Producer gets a full-time assistant. Everything starts with the script. No show can be a real success unless the script is sound. But numbers of free-lance writers work on each show, each one writing a different serial. Someone is needed to find the best writers for the show, co-ordinate their efforts, evaluate different story ideas, help writers to develop their ideas and cope with various script crises. Scripts prove to be too long or too short at the last moment, actors have difficulty with a scene or a line, writers fall ill and can't complete their assignments ... All this is another full-time job. Although the final decisions are his, the Producer will delegate most of the work directly concerned with the writing of the show to his Script Editor.

Although we've been referring above to the Producer as 'he', in fact the very first Producer of *Doctor Who* was a young woman called Verity Lambert. The first

Script Editor was David Whitaker, himself a very experienced television writer.

Immediately David Whitaker set to work to write a 'format'; notes about the series to guide possible writers.

Before long Anthony Coburn had been commissioned to write the first serial, in which the Doctor and his companions were to be carried back to the Stone Age.

Verity Lambert, meanwhile, had a very important decision to make. Who should play Doctor Who? She chose a very good character-actor called William Hartnell, then best known for playing crooks and army sergeants. It was something of a gamble. Hartnell had never before played anyone remotely like the Doctor. Still no more had anyone else!

Television, like any other business, is dominated by the question of money. The BBC's money comes, of course, from the licence fee paid by listeners and viewers. If you consider the wide range of the BBC's programmes, you will see that this money has to be divided between an enormous number of shows. *Doctor Who* was not a particularly important project. Its share of the BBC's money and resources was small, and had to be spread very thin.

Verity Lambert worked hard, looking for good but not expensive actors, and allocating her strictly limited resources between writers, actors, directors, scenery, costumes, make-up and all the hundreds of other things that go towards a television show. She even persuaded the BBC workshops to make complicated devices from odds and ends left over from other shows.

After many weeks of preparation the first episode of *Doctor Who* was transmitted. It was watched by two or three million viewers, a modest-sized audience for a modest little show.

The *second* serial started on 28 December 1963. It introduced some strange creatures called Daleks—and all at once, *Doctor Who* was launched on the road to success.

2

Enter the Daleks!

'Exterminate! Exterminate!' Probably no science-fiction
monster has ever caused so much interest and excite-
ment as the famous Daleks. Gliding along the metallic
corridors of their underground city on the planet Skaro,
or along London streets on one of their attempted invasions of Earth, squawking in electronic voices their
war-cry 'Exterminate! Exterminate!', they have
brought fear, terror and a great deal of pleasure to
millions of viewers.

The Daleks, who first appeared in the Doctor's second
adventure, were created by Terry Nation. But he almost
didn't write for *Doctor Who* at all. During the early
days, before the series was seen on the screen, Script
Editor David Whitaker had to think of writers for the
programme. Terry Nation was known mainly as a
comedy writer, but he had written one science-fiction
script which David Whitaker had seen and liked very
much. So David Whitaker sent a copy of the format to
Terry Nation's literary agent, inviting Nation to write
a *Doctor Who* serial. The agent sent on the format to
Terry Nation, who at the time was in Nottingham working on a stage comedy script for the late Tony Hancock.
Tony Hancock joked: 'How dare the BBC approach
a writer of your calibre to write for children's television!' That day, Nation telephoned his agent in London and told her he was really too busy to accept David
Whitaker's invitation.

But the job for Tony Hancock fell through, and

next morning the writer found himself on a train back to London—with no work. Remembering the invitation to write for *Doctor Who,* Nation telephoned his agent the moment he reached London. Had she turned down the offer yet? Luckily she hadn't, so Nation gladly accepted, and got to work. He first produced an outline of the story he had in mind. The Script Editor was delighted with it. The treatment had imagination, excellent characters and a driving story. It also had Daleks, but no one at that stage had any idea quite how popular these were going to be.

In his script, Nation described the Daleks like this: HIDEOUS MACHINE-LIKE CREATURES. THEY ARE LEGLESS, MOVING ON A ROUND BASE. THEY HAVE NO HUMAN FEATURES. A LENS ON A FLEXIBLE SHAFT ACTS AS AN EYE. ARMS WITH MECHANICAL GRIPS FOR HANDS. Raymond Cusick, a BBC designer, did some drawings of what he thought Daleks should look like, based on the description in the script. This first design, excellent at it was, proved to be too expensive for the budget. So Cusick, with two other design experts, Jack Kine and Bernard Wilkie, set to work to produce a simpler design. Together, they designed the familiar pepper-pot shape, inside which a very small actor could sit. The Dalek would be on castors, or tiny swivelling wheels, and would be driven along simply by the actor running his feet along the floor.

'The Daleks Came Alive!'

The drawings of the design were shown to Producer Verity Lambert, and to Script Editor David Whitaker. They were both rather disappointed by them. Still, everything in television has to be done to a deadline.

There was no time to ask the designers to think again. The design had to be accepted.

Six Daleks had to be made for Terry Nation's story, and when they were finished Verity Lambert was asked to come and look at them, and to bring along the actors who would sit in them. Not at all excited by the event, Verity went along with the actors to the BBC car park where the six Daleks were waiting. The designers started to explain to the actors how they must sit inside, and how to pull the levers that made the gun and eye-sticks go up and down. Then, suddenly, magic seemed to happen. As Verity says: 'The Daleks came alive. The actors inside started to chase each other around the car park, shouting from inside those pepper-pot domes "I am a Dalek! I am a Dalek!" We all wanted to get into them, and to become Daleks.'

What happened in that car park was soon to happen to millions of children all over Britain. All you had to do was to get a cardboard box, put it on your head, say 'Exterminate!' in a grating metallic voice, and you were a Dalek. In the months that followed the first Dalek story on television, all sorts of Dalek novelties came into the shops. You could buy Dalek sweets, toys, soap, slippers, Easter eggs and special Dalek fireworks. You could even have your bedroom decorated with Dalek wallpaper. The game of snakes and ladders became 'Doctor Who and the Daleks'. Two cinema films were made about the Daleks. British toy manufacturers were not quick enough to make all the Dalek toys that were wanted, so factories in Hong Kong made many of the toys that were sold here.

As well as the two cinema films, there was a Dalek stage show, and Terry Nation has the four Daleks from that production at his house in Kent. He frequently loans them for charity fêtes in the district, and people come from miles around just to look at the Daleks.

Terry Nation is the first to admit that the astonishing success of the Daleks took him completely by surprise. He was equally amazed at the long-running success of *Doctor Who*. How could this crazy fellow, who passed his time travelling all over the Galaxy in a Police Box, last more than a dozen episodes, he thought as he read the format.

When the boom was under way, Terry Nation was often asked by journalists how he thought of the name 'Dalek'. 'In a desperate attempt to satisfy them, I told them I was inspired by the letters on a volume of an encyclopaedia. But the fact is that no encyclopaedia in print covers those letters, DAL–LEK. Anyone checking the facts could have found me out.'

Nation himself doesn't really know where the name came from. As so often happens with writers, it just 'rolled off the typewriter'.

Why are the Daleks such a phenomenon? For Terry Nation the answer is simple. 'Kids love to be frightened. To them it's like creeping up to the top of the stairs in the dark, which is surely a healthy emotion.'

However, this can't be the whole explanation. The Doctor has faced many terrifying enemies in his long career, but none have ever had the instant and over-whelming appeal of the Daleks.

Perhaps another statement of Terry Nation's holds the real secret. 'The Daleks,' he says firmly, 'must always be totally *evil*.' Could this be the answer? Children, and adults too, for that matter, are always being urged to be *good*. To do things they don't really want to, and not to do the things they do! There is considerable appeal in the thought of a creature totally and utterly *bad*.

Whatever the reasons, the Daleks were an immediate

16

success. Soon Britain was Dalek-crazy, and the weekly audience for *Doctor Who* had doubled, and was steadily rising.

It would be a mistake to attribute *all* the success of *Doctor Who* to the Daleks. Although the Daleks have often returned to our screens, Dalek stories form only a small proportion of the total number of programmes. Nevertheless, like Sherlock Holmes and Professor Moriarty, like Chauvelin and the Scarlet Pimpernel, the Doctor and the Daleks are for ever linked. The Daleks gave the programme a tremendous boost in those crucial early days. The Doctor has good reason to be grateful to his deadliest opponents!

3

Who is the Doctor?

When the Doctor first appeared on our television screens his past was a complete mystery. We knew only that he was a traveller in Space and Time, and possibly a fugitive from his own people.

Over the years, a good deal more of the Doctor's background has emerged. In this chapter we shall attempt to piece together what we have learned.

What was the Doctor *like* in those early days? He appeared to be somewhere in his sixties, a little stiff and crotchety, but still spry, vigorous and alert. His frock-coat, check trousers and high stiff collar made him rather like the popular picture of an eccentric Victorian professor. He was accompanied by a young girl, Susan, who called him 'grandfather', and he travelled in a marvellous but sometimes erratic machine called the TARDIS.

Inside, the TARDIS is a fantastically advanced craft which can travel through Space and Time. The most astonishing thing about the TARDIS is the fact that it's bigger on the inside than on the outside—a fact which the Doctor sometimes explains by muttering crossly that it is 'dimensionally transcendental'. Although still very active, with a great appetite for knowledge and adventure, this first Doctor was already showing signs of his great age. He was sometimes querulous and irritable, impatient with those whose intelligence didn't match his own. He was capable of a kind of childish secretiveness and selfishness. In an early adventure, he endangered the lives of his companions by deliberately sabotaging his own TARDIS, because he wished to stay and explore a dangerous alien planet.

Despite his failings, the Doctor was still a formidable character. His quick wits and his courage carried him, together with a variety of companions, through numerous exciting adventures on Earth (past and future) and on many alien worlds.

Then, at the end of an adventure with the terrible Cybermen, the Doctor casually announced that his old body was beginning to 'wear out'. He collapsed into a coma, and his astonished companions saw him begin to change … When he recovered he was, literally, a different man.

For a start he looked much younger. Moreover, his temperament had changed with his appearance. *This* Doctor was a strange, elusive character, gentle and wayward with a whimsical charm. The arrogance of his previous incarnation had vanished and he was modest and unassuming. His clothes became more extravagant and eccentric, he played the flute, and sometimes he wore extraordinary hats. But beneath this rather clownish exterior, the Doctor's brilliant mind and forceful personality were unchanged, and in the time that followed this odd-looking little man was to save the day in many a terrifying crisis.

The Doctor retained this form through many adventures. Then, at last, he encountered the terrible War Lords, who were attempting a Galactic conspiracy so vast and terrifying that even the Doctor had to ask for help. It was now that we began to learn a little more about his past. The Doctor, it appeared, was a kind of renegade, a maverick member of an immensely advanced and powerful race. The Time Lords had the power to travel in Space and Time, as well as to regenerate their own bodies when threatened by old age or illness. It was a part of their philosophy that they must use their powers to observe the affairs of the Universe, but never to intervene. The Doctor, however, was convinced that it was necessary to at least *try* to right some of the Galaxy's many wrongs. He had stolen the TARDIS and fled to roam the Universe, struggling against evil when and wherever he encountered it. But in this final crisis, he was forced to turn to his own people for help, even though he knew that to do so would mean recapture.

The conspiracy of the War Lords was frustrated, but in the process the Doctor was taken prisoner by his own people and put on trial before the High Court of the Time Lords. Unrepentant, he made a moving speech, claiming that it was the moral duty of the Time Lords to help the weak and oppressed, to use their powers to struggle against evil as he had done.

Although he was found guilty, the Doctor's plea was not without its effect. His sentence was a comparatively light one, a period of exile on the planet Earth in the twentieth century time zone. It is interesting to note that the Doctor's rebellion brought about a gradual shift in the policy of the High Council of the Time Lords. From this point they were to intervene more and more in the affairs of the Galaxy, often using the Doctor as their unwilling agent.

The Doctor's exile was, in itself, an example of this change. The Time Lords must have been aware that it would coincide with a time of great crisis for Earth. Immediately upon his arrival the Doctor became involved in the first Auton invasion, and many more alien attacks on Earth were to follow.

As part of the Doctor's sentence, the Time Lords decided there should be yet another change in his appearance. The Doctor who arrived on Earth was very different from the comic little rebel who had defied the Court of the Time Lords.

This new Doctor was a more obviously heroic figure than in his previous incarnations. He was tall, lean and elegant, with a handsome lined face, and a shock of white hair. His taste in clothes was flamboyant, running to frilled shirts, velvet smoking jackets and elaborate cloaks. He was very much the man of action, dashing, impulsive and with a ready charm. Although he never carried weapons, apart from his multi-purpose sonic screwdriver, he was an expert in Venusian Aikido, one of the few two-armed beings to master this most deadly of Intergalactic Martial Arts.

One of the new Doctor's strongest characteristics was a passion for all kinds of gadgetry, and for any new and original form of transport. His souped-up Edwardian roadster 'Bessie' was a typical example. Later the Doctor acquired his 'Whomobile', a futuristic-looking vehicle something between a racing car and a flying saucer, with the ability to take to the air in times of crisis. In the course of his adventures, this Doctor drove speedboats, hovercraft, and even a one-man helicopter.

Perhaps the most extraordinary adventure of this period involved the Doctor in a confrontation with his two former selves. The Time Lords decided that no less than three Doctors were needed to deal with the renegade Time Lord Omega, and lifted the Doctor's earlier selves from their proper Time Streams so that he could literally help himself.

The collaboration began amiably enough but it didn't stay like that. The third Doctor clashed immediately with his second incarnation, and although they eventually succeeded in defeating Omega, their collaboration was a stormy one, with the first Doctor often acting as peacemaker.

It was as a result of this particular adventure that the Time Lords lifted the Doctor's sentence of exile, restoring his freedom to roam Time and Space once more. Ironically, this new freedom eventually led to the end of the Doctor's third incarnation.

On a trip to Metebelis Three, famous blue planet of the Acteon Galaxy, the Doctor acquired one of the planet's blue crystals as a souvenir. Unfortunately, this particular crystal formed an important part of the plans of the giant Spiders, ruthless rulers of the planet. Returning to Metebelis with the crystal, the Doctor was forced to enter the cave of the Great One, their all-powerful Ruler, and although he succeeded in destroying her, his body became riddled with the deadly alien radiation of her cave. There was only one way to save his life—the Doctor had to change his appearance yet again...

And so the Doctor entered on his fourth incarnation, looking as different from the first three as they did from each other. Still tall and sharp-featured, he now seemed much younger, with a mop of curly brown hair and a bubbling eccentric vitality. But in spite of this difference in appearance, the latest Doctor showed many of the qualities of the three that had gone before. The strong will and brilliant scientific brain of the first, the inconsequential humour of the second, the warmth and charm of the third. A strange mixture of contradictory qualities, genius and clown, hero and buffoon, he was well equipped to face the many exciting adventures that lay before him.

Much has changed about the Doctor over the years, but much has remained the same. Despite the superficial differences in appearance, at heart, or rather at *hearts* (the Doctor has two), his character is remarkably consistent.

He is still impulsive, idealistic, ready to risk his life for a worthy cause. He still hates tyranny and oppression, and anything that is anti-life. He never gives in, and he never gives up, however overwhelming the odds against him.

The Doctor believes in good and fights evil. Though often caught up in violent situations, he is a man of peace. He is never cruel or cowardly.

In fact, to put it simply, the Doctor is a hero. These days there aren't so many of them around . . .

4

Tom Baker is Doctor Who

The affairs of *Doctor Who* had reached crisis. After five years in the role, Jon Pertwee, the star of the show, had reluctantly decided it was time to move on. He wanted to return to the wider world of stage, variety, films and radio that had been the mainstream of his career. The starring role in a long-running TV series carries its own problems for an actor. On the one hand he has success, prestige and an assured regular income. But there are dangers. An actor can become too identified with a particular TV role. By the time he does decide to leave, or the show comes to an end, the public refuses to accept him as anyone else—a grave handicap for his future career. Determined to avoid this trap, Pertwee made his decision—he would leave *Doctor Who* at the peak of his success. Two other members of the *Doctor Who* team had come to the same decision. Producer Barry Letts and Script Editor Terrance Dicks had both joined the show at the same time as Jon Pertwee. After five exciting but demanding years, they too felt it was time for a change. Barry Letts was keen to return to his first love, directing, for a spell. (He later took up an appointment as Producer of the BBC's Classic Serials). Terrance Dicks wanted to return to writing his own scripts, rather than editing other peoples', and was now increasingly involved with Target's *Doctor Who* paperback series. Everyone felt that a five-year era was coming to its natural end. It was time for a new team to take over.

Two of the three vacancies were filled without much

24

delay. Bob Holmes, an experienced television script-writer, and a regular contributor to the programme over the previous five years, became the new Script Editor. Philip Hinchcliffe, recently moved over from ITV, was to become the new Producer.

But the third, and to the public the most important vacancy, was still unfilled. Who was going to be the new Doctor Who? One of the many ways in which *Doctor Who* is unique is that its lead actor periodically changes. To replace the lead in any show is always a risk. If the show is a success, the actor now playing the part will have built up a tremendously loyal following. Will these fans transfer their affections to his successor? Or will they resent him?

Doctor Who had already brought off this incredibly difficult trick twice, each time with tremendous success. Many viewers thought Jon Pertwee was the best Doctor in the programme's long history. Could the trick be pulled off a third time?

The search was lengthy and intensive, and for a long time unsuccessful. Many names were considered and discussed, some famous, some still unknown, but none seemed exactly right. Meanwhile the rumour of Pert-wee's departure had leaked out, and the press were de-manding the name of the new Doctor. And time was moving on. The part would *have* to be cast soon, if the new actor was to begin rehearsing the first show of the next season.

At this point there came a message from Bill Slater, the BBC's Head of Serials. If they hadn't actually de-cided on the new Doctor, would they care to take a look at an actor called Tom Baker? He was an experienced theatre actor who had appeared in several films, winning excellent reviews for his portrayal of Rasputin, the famous 'Mad Monk' in the film *Nicholas and Alex-*

andra. In his latest film *The Golden Voyage of Sinbad* he was once more playing the villain.

Barry Letts and Terrance Dicks took an afternoon off from the office and went to see the film. Tom Baker played the wicked magician, a man worn out by the exercise of his own evil powers. Each spell left him a little older and more exhausted, and he was searching desperately for the Fountain of Youth to renew his failing strength. The character was sympathetic as well as villainous, and it was impossible not to feel saddened at his eventual defeat. By the time they left the cinema, they felt sure that their search was over. Soon afterwards, it was announced that Tom Baker was to be the new Doctor Who.

Tom Baker's background is as interesting and unusual as the man himself. He was born and educated in Liverpool. At the age of sixteen, he joined a monastic order on the Isle of Skye, spending the next four years as a monk. But this important decision had been taken very early, and as the years went by Tom Baker became less and less certain of his vocation. At the age of twenty he left the monastery with a new and very different ambition. He wanted to become an actor.

At this point the Government stepped in. He was called up for National Service, and spent the next two years in the Army. Not until this was over was he free to begin the long struggle to establish himself.

First he went to drama school. Then began the next stage, working in various repertory theatres around the country. Gradually his name became known, and he eventually got a job with the famous York Repertory Theatre, moving from there to the National Theatre Company, where he stayed for two and a half years. Not long after this his film career began. Laurence Olivier recommended him for the part of Rasputin in *Nicholas and Alexandra*. He also appeared in *Canterbury Tales*, *Vault of Horror* and *The Golden Voyage of Sinbad*—which is where we came in!

By now Tom Baker has made the part of Doctor Who his own. The long trailing scarf, the floppy wide-brimmed hat, the mop of curly hair and the wide-eyed penetrating stare—all these mean Doctor Who to millions of viewers. Hundreds of children turn up to see him at Target book-signing sessions. The fourth incarnation of *Doctor Who* has been launched on what looks like a long and successful career.

5

The Three Doctors

The First Doctor Who was William Hartnell

William Hartnell became an actor at the age of sixteen, when he joined Sir Frank Benson's Shakespearean Company as a general dog's-body, call-boy, assistant stage manager, property manager, and assistant lighting director. Sometimes he was allowed to play small walk-on parts, and in two years with that company, working day and night, he learnt a great deal about the theatre and about acting.

At the age of eighteen he started to tour the country as an actor, playing in theatres the length and breadth of Great Britain. Then he started to get jobs understudying in London's West End theatres. (In a stage play, all the actors and actresses have understudies, who have learnt their parts. If an actor is taken ill, the understudy plays his part that night.) He became known as an actor of farce. He understudied such great actors as Ralph Lynn and Ernest Truex, and then played their parts himself when their plays left the West End and went on tour of the provincial cities.

He got into films in the 1930s, playing comedy parts in 'quickies'—short films, made very cheaply in two or three weeks of filming. For his first leading part in one of these films, he was paid £60. Today, an actor playing the leading part in a film would be paid thousands of pounds. However, his whole acting career changed in 1943 when the famous film producer Sir Carol Reed asked him to play a tough Army sergeant in the film *The*

Way Ahead. This film was enormously succcessful, and so was William Hartnell. But it meant that for the next twenty years no producer could forget the way he played that tough Army sergeant. He had become type-cast, and from then on was offered only tough-guy parts such as sergeants, prison officers, grim detectives and criminals. Even when he started to work in television, and got into the very successful *Army Game* comedy series, he was not allowed to play a comedy character. They made him the tough sergeant-major.

Then he landed a part in the film *This Sporting Life.* Verity Lambert saw the film, and was greatly impressed by Hartnell's performance. She decided to ask him to become the first Doctor Who, and contacted his agent. The agent telephoned Hartnell and told him, 'I wouldn't normally have suggested it to you, Bill, to work in children's television, but it sounds the sort of character part you have been longing to play.' Hartnell wasn't too keen on the idea, but agreed to meet Verity Lambert.

He said of that meeting: 'The moment this brilliant young producer, Miss Verity Lambert, started telling me about Doctor Who, I was hooked.' From the very first he was sure the series would be successful.

William Hartnell played Doctor Who for over three years, finally retiring for reasons of health. He spent the last few years of his life in a tiny country cottage in Mayfield, Sussex. During those years people still wrote to him as Doctor Who, or called at his cottage to see him. Sadly, he is no longer with us, but part of him lives on in the immortal Doctor Who, the character he created so brilliantly, so many years ago.

Patrick Troughton was born in London in 1920, and was educated at Mill Hill Public School. He started his career by going to the Embassy School of Acting, at Swiss Cottage in London, which was run by Eileen Thorndyke, sister of the famous Dame Sybil Thorndyke. He won a scholarship from there to go to the Leighton Rallius Studio for actors at the John Drew Memorial Theatre in Long Island, USA. He was in America when the Second World War broke out, and returned to Britain on a neutral Belgian ship. It crossed the Atlantic safely, then just off Portland Bill, in sight of England, it hit an enemy mine and sank. Troughton was one of the lucky ones to escape in the life-boats.

He joined the Tonbridge Repertory Company in 1939, and was acting there for a year. In June 1940, he joined the Royal Navy. First he was in destroyers, protecting East Coast convoys from enemy submarine attack. Then he was transferred to motor gun boats, and was given his own command just after the Allied invasion of Normandy. He was demobilised from the Navy in March 1945, and joined the Amersham Repertory Company.

Troughton first got into television in 1948, when it had just started again after the war. Since then he has played an enormous number of dramatic parts on our screens.

He was making a film in Ireland called *The Viking Queen* when asked if he would like to become the second Doctor Who. At first he didn't want to do it, he felt it was not the right type of part for him. Whenever possible, he watched the show with his children, and he loved the way that William Hartnell played the Doctor. But it was not, he thought, right for him. Still, the BBC managed to persuade him, and he accepted.

The next question was, *how* he was to play the Doctor. 'Why not play it like Charlie Chaplin,' said Sydney Newman, the BBC's Head of Drama at that time, 'a sort of cosmic hobo.' And that, in fact, was how Patrick Troughton played Doctor Who for the next three years.

Of his time as the Doctor, Patrick Troughton says: 'Of all my years as an actor, I think these were the happiest. I particularly enjoyed acting with Frazer Hines, who played Jamie. We never once had a cross word all the time we worked together. Also Innes Lloyd, the Producer when I started, and Peter Bryant were great to work for. I had a lot of fun.'

In return, Patrick Troughton gave the millions of viewers a lot of fun. He was enormously popular as the Doctor. But after three years he felt very firmly that enough was enough. Patrick Troughton had always been, and always wanted to be, an actor rather than a personality. Someone who could transform himself completely, get 'under the skin' of many different characters. His interpretation of the Doctor was only one of the parts within his range. He left the series to return to a more varied world.

Patrick Troughton still turns up regularly on your screens. But it's quite possible, such is his acting skill, that in some snarling villain, sympathetic hero, or richly comic character, you won't recognise the man who was once Doctor Who.

Jon Pertwee was The Third Doctor Who

Many people in the world of show business were surprised when Jon Pertwee was cast as the third Doctor Who. But most surprised was Pertwee himself!

31

Although already famous, Jon Pertwee's reputation was made mainly in the field of what is usually called Light Entertainment, and more particularly in comedy. A polished radio performer with an incredible range of funny voices, he was one of the original cast in that long-running radio comedy series, *The Navy Lark*. Years before he had been a regular in another radio show, Eric Barker's *Waterlogged Spa*.

As a cabaret artist he delights audiences all over Britain, and he has made a number of successful LP records. He has appeared in West End stage productions, such as *A Funny Thing Happened on the Way to the Forum*, and the long-running comedy hit, *There's A Girl In My Soup*. He is also a talented folk-singer and guitarist.

When Jon Pertwee heard the rumour that Patrick Troughton was leaving, the wild thought came into his head that *he* might be the new Doctor Who. But would anyone really consider him for what was basically a serious dramatic role? He spoke to his agent, who agreed that it was a long-shot, but worth a try. The agent telephoned Peter Bryant, then Producer of the programme, and hesitantly made the suggestion. There was a stunned silence. Then the Producer said, 'Let me tell you the name at the top of my short-list!' It was, of course, Jon Pertwee.

Jon Pertwee chose to play the Doctor as an extension of his own character. 'Doctor Who is me,' he said at the time, 'or I am Doctor Who. I played him straight from myself.' The change of Doctors was soon reflected on the television screen. William Hartnell's Doctor, and to some extent Patrick Troughton's, had been *thinkers*, tending to leave the rough-stuff to younger and brawnier characters in the story. Pertwee's Doctor was a man of action, always ready to tackle the villains in person. Soon

32

the tall, elegant figure in the flowing cape became firmly established as the new Doctor Who.

Another area in which the actor's tastes affected the series was that of transport. Jon Pertwee is genuinely fascinated by any machine that moves, perferably very fast, on land, in the water or in the air. Cars, motor-bikes, speedboats and planes feature largely in his life. This Doctor soon acquired his own transport, a souped-up Edwardian roadster known as 'Bessie'.

Bessie was followed by the Whomobile, a strange flying saucer-like vehicle with the ability, on television at least, to take to the air in moments of emergency. Typically, Pertwee helped to design the machine himself. Other vehicles—speedboats, gyrocopters, even a one-man hovercraft, began to appear in the series.

Jon Pertwee played Doctor Who for five action-packed years, giving the series a new image and a new lease of life. He enjoyed every minute of it—but eventually the time came when he too felt that he was in danger of being trapped by his own success, that it was time to move on. Another era in the Doctor Who story had drawn to a close.

6

Monsters Galore—and the Master!

One of the many fascinations of *Doctor Who* is the wide variety of monstrous alien life-forms, mostly hostile, encountered by the Doctor. Some of these monsters have returned to the attack time and again, becoming a regular feature of the series. The Daleks, for example, have already had a chapter to themselves. Here are some of the Doctor's monstrous enemies—you can read more about his encounters with them in the *Travels of Doctor Who* section.

The Cybermen

These silver giants, once humanoids in form, sought immortality by means of the science of cybernetics—the reproduction of machine functions in living beings. Gradually they replaced parts of their flesh and blood bodies with metal and plastic.

When the process was finally complete the Cybermen were formidable indeed. Their giant bodies had the strength of ten men. Their built-in respiratory system allowed them to exist without protective suits in the airless vacuum of space. They were immune to cold and heat. But all these gains were balanced by terrible losses. In their final form the Cybermen had no feelings. Love, hate, fear had no meaning for them. Worse still, they had no scruples, no pity, no conscience. Their one aim was power.

34

They made a number of attempts to conquer the planet Earth, all foiled by the Doctor, who also encountered them in Space, and on alien planets.

The Cybermen are humanoid in shape, giant silver figures about seven feet tall. Their terrifying heads are made of silver metal with blank round eyes, thin cut-out slits for mouths and handle-like projections in place of ears. They made use of a number of specially developed Cyberweapons, most striking of which is the Cybermat, a kind of metal rat with a variety of unpleasant uses.

The Cybermen appear in the Target books *Doctor Who and the Cybermen, Doctor Who and the Tenth Planet* and *Doctor Who and the Revenge of the Cybermen.*

The Ice Warriors

The first Ice Warrior was found buried deep in the ice at a period when Earth was in the grip of a second Ice Age. The huge helmeted figure, frozen into a solid block of ice, was at first taken for the preserved body of some long-dead Viking warrior.

Once the creature was revived, the name proved appropriate enough. The Ice Warrior was the captain of a buried spaceship, a member of a savagely militaristic race originating on the planet Mars. Green in colour, and a good eight feet tall, the Ice Warriors have massive, crested, helmet-like heads. Their armoured bodies form a massive protective shell, and the powerful arms end not in hands or claws, but in huge metallic clamps.

A tubular device projects from the right forearm—a built-in sonic gun. The Ice Warriors are masters of sonic technology, invulnerable to most forms of attack, and well able to defend themselves. Luckily for the Doctor they have one great weakness. Used to the bleak cold of their own dying planet, they are unable to stand heat, a fact which the Doctor has more than once used to defeat them on Earth, and on the barbaric planet of Peladon.

You can read about the Ice Warriors in *Doctor Who and the Ice Warriors* and *Doctor Who and the Curse of Peladon*.

The Yeti

First encountered by the Doctor in Tibet, the Yeti appear to be living creatures, the famous Abominable Snowmen of the Himalayas. The massive bodies, covered in shaggy brown fur, are so broad that the creatures seem squat and lumpy despite their towering height. Their huge hairy hands and black muzzles are gorilla-like, their red eyes and yellow fangs like those of a grizzly bear.

But as the Doctor soon discovered in Tibet, beneath the brown fur is the metal-framed body of a robot. The Yeti were created by the Great Intelligence, a formless mind drifting in space, as part of its plans for the conquest of Earth. They are controlled by silver spheres set into their chests. Once he became aware of this, the Doctor was able to control the robots. During a second attack on Earth, when Yeti were roaming the tunnels of the London Underground, the Doctor was even able to turn one of these servants of the Intelligence into a kind of ally.

The Yeti appear in *Doctor Who and the Abominable Snowmen* and *Doctor Who and the Web of Fear*.

Like the Yeti, the Autons are really living weapons, constructed in this case by the Nestenes, disembodied alien invaders with a sinister affinity for all forms of plastic. The Autons are man-shaped and come in several designs. The basic fighting Auton wears rough overalls and has a blank unfinished face, the features lumpy and crude. The elaborate models resemble shop-window dummies, with inhumanly handsome faces.

Most sophisticated of all are the Replicas, accurate copies of real people, able, for a time at least, to pass as the originals. All three models of Autons have one thing in common. Their hinged hands can drop away at the wrist to reveal a Nestene energy-gun, capable of sending out a powerful energy-bolt that kills humans on impact.

The most terrifying shape of the Nestene consciousness and their only 'true' form, is a giant many-tentacled monster, something between spider, crab and octopus, with a single huge eye, blazing with malignant hatred. This was designed to contain the Nestene mind during their final invasions—invasions which, luckily for us, were foiled by the Doctor.

In their second invasion of the Earth the Nestenes, this time helped by the evil Master, a renegade Time Lord, increased the range of their weapons. The Doctor and his friends found themselves menaced once again by the Autons, now in the form of carnival figures with huge grinning heads.

But the Nestenes also attacked with plastic armchairs, a killer doll, a telephone flex, and most deadly of all, innocent looking plastic daffodils, which spat out a choking plastic film.

The Autons appear in *Doctor Who and the Auton Invasion* and *Doctor Who and the Terror of the Autons*.

Silurians and Sea Devils

The Silurians are huge intelligent reptiles, survivors of a reptilian civilisation which flourished on Earth before the rise of man. Aroused from their long hibernation they attempted to re-conquer the planet, seeing man only as an 'upstart ape'. These giant green reptiles walked upright like men, but that was the only resemblance. Their ridged, crested heads had huge flat ears. A glowing third eye in the centre of the forehead gives them strange hypnotic powers.

The Sea Devils are members of the same species, though the head formation is different, with something of the look of a giant tortoise. They are marine creatures, based deep beneath the sea, and their attempt to conquer the Earth started with a series of attacks on shipping.

See the books *Doctor Who and the Cave Monsters* and *Doctor Who and the Sea Devils*.

The Sontarans

Short, squat and immensely powerful, the Sontarans look like some hideous goblin or troll from Earth's ancient legends. Small red eyes glare from a massive dome-shaped head and the wide mouth is an almost lipless slit.

In reality, however, the Sontarans are an advanced alien space-travelling species with one consuming interest—warfare!

Despite his humanoid form, the Master certainly merits a place among the monsters—in fact he himself would probably insist on it!

Not that there is anything monstrous in his appearance. The Master appears to be a man of medium size, powerfully built and tremendously strong. His large, dark eyes and neatly pointed beard give him a slightly foreign air. He has a deep warm voice, and possesses a charm that can be literally hypnotic.

Like the Doctor, the Master is a renegade Time Lord. But while the Doctor is merely independent and a little erratic, the Master is dedicatedly evil. He loves chaos and disaster for its own sake, will start a war for the sheer fun of it, and likes nothing better than to make a bad situation worse.

His one ambition is to destroy the Doctor, who has foiled so many of his evil plans. To this end the Master has joined forces with a wide variety of alien allies—Nestenes, Sea Devils, Axons, even the dreaded Daleks.

Always defeated, he always escapes to try again. The Doctor admits to a kind of unwilling admiration for the Master. Not that he approves of him, of course, the fellow hasn't got a single redeeming feature, but the cosmos would certainly be a duller place without him ... You can read about the Master's evil schemes in *Doctor Who and the Terror of the Autons, Doctor Who and the Doomsday Weapon, Doctor Who and the Daemons* and *Doctor Who and the Sea Devils*.

7

The Men from UNIT

UNIT, the United Nations Intelligence Taskforce, was created specifically to protect the planet Earth from extra-terrestial invasion. Once mankind had succeeded in sending satellites into space, and in setting foot upon the moon, we attracted the attention of a number of hostile alien species. Fearing perhaps that we would soon come out into space to challenge them, several alien races launched attacks on Earth, determined to lose no time in crushing this upstart species called Man.

Based on United Nations H.Q. in Geneva, the new organisation has branches all over the world. Each consists of a small, highly trained force of soldiers and scientists, under the command of a senior officer.

Brigadier Alastair Lethbridge-Stewart

'*Chap with wings. Five rounds rapid, fire!*' This typically cool, clipped order was once given by the Commanding Officer of the British branch of UNIT, Brigadier Alastair Lethbridge-Stewart, faced with yet another alien horror. Although thoroughly anglicised by public school and Sandhurst, the Brigadier comes of an old Scottish family with a long military tradition. Before his transfer to Intelligence duties, he served for a time in a famous Highland regiment, and has occasionally been known to wear the kilt.

In manner and appearance, the Brigadier is everyone's idea of the typical British Officer, with abrupt manner, clipped voice, and neatly trimmed moustache.

But is would be a mistake to assume that he is some kind of brainless Colonel Blimp. The conventional manner conceals a keen and flexible mind, broadened even more by his many encounters with alien species, and particularly by his long and often stormy association with the Doctor.

The two first met during the crisis of the Web of Fear, when the Great Intelligence was using Yeti to terrorise London. Soon after these events UNIT was formed. Colonel Lethbridge-Stewart, promoted to Brigadier, was placed in command of the British section. One of his first tasks was to resist an invasion by Cybermen, and the Doctor turned up in time to give the Brigadier a great deal of assistance.

Later still, the first Auton invasion coincided with the Doctor's change in appearance and exile to Earth by the Time Lords. At first the Brigadier failed to recognise his old friend, but once convinced that the new Doctor really was the same person, he gladly accepted his help, persuading the Doctor to remain as UNIT's Scientific Adviser once the invasion was defeated.

This was the beginning of a long association. Very different in temperament, the Doctor and the Brigadier are often at loggerheads over the *way* to tackle some specific problem, but beneath all the grumbling and the occasional fireworks, a very real friendship exists between them.

When the Doctor's exile was ended by the Time Lords, after the extraordinary affair of the Three Doctors, his connection with UNIT became more tenuous. The Brigadier had a fresh source of complaint in the Doctor's undeniable tendency to go haring off to the far corners of the Galaxy on the slightest excuse. In addition, the Brigadier has had to come to terms with yet another change in the Doctor's appearance.

Since every change in appearance produces an equivalent change in character, the Brigadier had to get used to an even wilder and more eccentric version of his old friend. However, after the terrifying adventure of the Giant Robot, the Brigadier realised that despite the surface changes the Doctor was essentially the same, and the old friendship became stronger than ever. Now, in his fourth incarnation, the Doctor's wanderlust seems to have increased. These days the Brigadier is seeing rather less of his old friend. But however much the Brigadier may grumble at the Doctor's increasing tendency to disappear in the TARDIS, he feels confident that in a real emergency, like the recent problem of the Loch Ness Monster, the Doctor will always appear in time to sort things out.

Captain Michael Yates

Mike Yates served as the Brigadier's loyal number two for many years. A slight, wiry young man with a thin, sensitive face, he is quite unlike the usual idea of an army officer.

Captain Yates was perhaps too sensitive, and it was this which led to his downfall. Although he met the threat of a number of alien invasions with unflinching courage, the continual strain on his nerves inevitably had its effect. During the adventure of the Green Death, his mind was, for some time, taken over by BOSS, a megalomaniac computer that had developed a will of its own. The Doctor managed to return him to normal by using the powers of the strange blue crystal from the planet Metebelis Three.

The Brigadier sent Captain Yates on a spell of extended sick leave. Unfortunately, this well-meant action was the cause of further trouble. Bored and at a loose end, Mike Yates wandered into one of the meetings of the Save Planet Earth Society, and came under the influence of its founder, Sir Charles Grover. He was soon caught up in Grover's plan to reverse the course of Time and bring back a Golden Age. Throughout the mystery of the Dinosaur Invasion, Yates was actually working against the Doctor and UNIT, sabotaging their attempts to get at the truth.

When this was revealed, and the invasion over, the Brigadier had no alternative but to dismiss Captain Yates from UNIT. Partly because of his past good services, partly to avoid a scandal, no charges were preferred and he was discreetly invalided out.

But Mike Yates' involvement with the Doctor was by no means over. In search of some kind of personal salvation, he joined a meditation centre set up in the English countryside by exiled Tibetan monks. He soon realised something very strange indeed was going on. Although he couldn't summon up the courage to call UNIT, he did contact Sarah Jane Smith. Through her the Doctor became involved in the adventure of the Planet of the Spiders, which was to lead to the end of his third incarnation. In the courage he showed in this terrifying business, Mike Yates made full amends for his previous mistakes.

Warrant Officer Benton

Unlike the rather complex Captain Yates, W.O. Benton (previously Sergeant Benton) is exactly what he seems, a big, tough soldier who gets on with the job. No great thinker, as he would be the first to admit, he looks to the

Brigadier and the Doctor for his orders, and is unswervingly loyal to both.

After many years service in the rank of Sergeant, he was promoted to Warrant Officer, the army's senior non-commissioned rank, and is now entitled to be addressed as 'Mister'. Mr Benton has faced a wide variety of alien horrors during his service with UNIT, meeting them all with the same unflinching courage. Perhaps his most exciting adventure was that of The Three Doctors, where he found himself taking a trip to an anti-matter world in the TARDIS—and coping with Three Doctors at the same time!

Harry Sullivan

Latest addition to the strength of UNIT is Harry Sullivan. He is a burly young man with blue eyes, curly hair and a square jaw, and looks exactly like the fearless hero of an old-fashioned boy's adventure story.

Like the Brigadier, Harry is a pretty conventional figure. He is a keen rugger player and a first-class boxer. After taking his medical degree he served for many years as a Naval Doctor. However, there's an adventurous streak in Harry Sullivan and it led him to apply for a posting to the unorthodox world of UNIT.

He met the Doctor at the beginning of his fourth incarnation, and was immediately caught up in the affair of the Giant Robot. It was after this that Harry rashly accepted the Doctor's offer of a trip in the TARDIS, and found himself whirled away on a series of adventures that involved him with Cybermen, Sontarans and Daleks. Harry didn't get back to Earth until the Doctor returned to deal with the menace of the Loch Ness Monster. Now that his feet are on firm ground again, he plans to stay there for a while!

8

The Good Companions

The Doctor has had no shortage of company on his trips around the Universe. When we first met him, he was travelling with Susan, whom he referred to as his 'grand-daughter', though it is possible that this was simply a title of affection. In the Doctor's first adventure he picked up Ian and Barbara, two teachers from Susan's school, whirling them away to the Stone Age. Other travellers in the TARDIS included Vicki, survivor of a crashed spaceship, Steven, a spaceship pilot, Ben, a cockney sailor, and Polly, a scientist's secretary. Later companions were Jamie, a tough young Highlander picked up during the Jacobite Rebellion, Victoria, the daughter of a nineteenth-century scientist, and Zoe, a computer operator from a space station.

Not all these companions were in the TARDIS at one and the same time, of course, though they often overlapped, particularly in the early days. It's just as well the TARDIS is dimensionally transcendental, or it would have been uncomfortably crowded in there at times!

Fortunately, from time to time people left the Doctor's 'crew'. Some the Doctor actually managed to get back to where they'd been picked up. Others decided for various reasons of their own to leave the TARDIS and settle down, though not always on the planet or in the time from which they'd set off.

Susan, the Doctor's 'grand-daughter', married a young freedom fighter after the Dalek invasion of Earth. Victoria was adopted by a childless couple in a scientific age long after her own Victorian times.

Jamie and Zoe, the last two companions of the Doctor's second incarnation, were perhaps most fortunate of all. They were returned to their own places and times by the Time Lords, and were able to take up their original lives again.

When the Doctor was exiled to Earth, the number of his companions became fewer. His first colleague at UNIT was Liz Shaw, a Cambridge scientist who soon left UNIT to resume her research work. After that, the Doctor's assistant was the diminutive Jo Grant, who accompanied him on several trips in the TARDIS when the Time Lords allowed him to get it moving again. Jo eventually married a brilliant young scientist and went off on an expedition up the Amazon with him.

The Doctor's next companion was to be with him through two incarnations. Sarah Jane Smith, an independently minded freelance journalist, stowed away on board the TARDIS in quest of a story and was carried back into the medieval past. Once involved with the Doctor she accompanied him on many adventures, on Earth and on other worlds.

Like the Brigadier, Sarah was present when the Doctor's body, riddled with deadly alien radiation, changed to the form in which we know him today. She also had to get used to an old friend with a new face. Once she had adjusted to the change they became good friends again. Sarah became the Doctor's constant companion, for ever swearing that she would never set foot in the TARDIS again, always unable to resist the Doctor's plea to accompany him just one more time ...

9

Some Regulars—Old and New

In television, this is the term for actors or actresses who play recurring characters in a series. There isn't room to mention all those who have made such a contribution to the programme over the years. However, here are some of the names behind some of the faces.

Elisabeth Sladen plays Sarah Jane Smith. She went to Drama School in Liverpool and did most of her early stage work in the Manchester area. Moving to London, she began appearing on television in such shows as *Some Mothers Do 'Ave 'Em* and *Z Cars*, but *Doctor Who* was the first time she appeared regularly on TV.

She says she doesn't mind big monsters like the Daleks, but hates what she calls 'creepies' like the scuttling rat-like Cybermats. And she admits that her character, Sarah Jane Smith, does need a bit of protection. 'She thinks she can stand on her own feet, and she'll always have a bash at things. But somebody normally ends up telling her she's totally wrong—and it's usually the Doctor.'

The Brigadier and Co.

Nicholas Courtney plays the Brigadier. He is one of the few actors who has appeared with all *four* Doctors. Even before his first appearance as Colonel Lethbridge-Stewart, he played a sort of space-age James Bond in a very early serial with William Hartnell.

The son of a diplomat, Nicholas Courtney was born in Egypt and grew up in France, Egypt and Kenya. He has worked in films, on stage and on television, playing all sorts of parts, though he does seem to specialise in army officers! His main concern in playing the Brigadier is to convey a real human being. 'I try to make him endearing, to get some fun into the action. I don't want him to look a twit.'

The Army themselves are pretty happy with Nicholas Courtney's characterisation. In fact a Senior Army Officer once told the Producer, 'Best thing about your show is the Brigadier. We've got lots of young Brigadiers *exactly* like that!'

Richard Franklyn plays Captain Yates. He really was an army officer for a while, a lieutenant in the Rifle Brigade. He left the army to become an actor and went to RADA (The Royal Academy of Dramatic Art, the actors' training school). He then joined the Century Theatre Company, where he played a wide variety of parts, and also swept the stage! Although he has often appeared on television, most of his acting experience has been in the theatre, particularly in classical roles. Being in *Doctor Who* is very interesting, he says—and *very* different from Shakespeare.

John Levene plays Warrant Officer Benton. He had no formal training as an actor, but worked his way up from being an 'extra', one of the non-speaking artists who appear in the background.

He enjoys working in *Doctor Who* enormously, though he complains jokingly that *his* lines are always cut if a show is running too long. His role as the good-looking Benton brings him quite a bit of fan mail, once from the entire female staff of a factory.

Ian Marter plays Harry Sullivan. Like Nicholas Courtney, Ian Marter once appeared in *Doctor Who* in another role. He played a young merchant Navy officer in a show called *Carnival of Monsters*. And it was as a result of this that he was offered the role of Harry Sullivan. Before joining *Doctor Who* Ian Marter had played several seasons with the Bristol Old Vic. He has appeared on TV in *Crown Court* and on the stage in *Conduct Unbecoming* and *Abelard and Heloise*.

The Master Villain

Roger Delgado played the Master. His rather sinister good looks were inherited from a French mother and a Spanish father, but he was also proud of being a true Cockney, born within the sound of Bow Bells.

He appeared in a tremendous number of films, television plays and stage plays, almost invariably as the villain. But even villains have their fans. During the filming of *The Daemons*, the Director asked onlooking children to boo and hiss the Master when he was recaptured by UNIT. But instead the audience insisted on cheering the Master.

Like many of those actors who specialise in playing black-hearted villains, Roger Delgado was in real life the kindest and gentlest of men. His tragic death in a car accident some years ago was a loss to the acting profession, and to all his many friends.

Some more Companions

Carol Ann Ford played Susan, the Doctor's granddaughter. She thinks she was cast because they wanted a good screamer. She certainly did an awful lot of screaming in the years that followed. She recalls that in the beginning *Doctor Who* was intended to be more scientific and educational, and less 'monstery'. But the monsters soon took over.

Peter Purves played Steven, the space pilot. He once attended a *Doctor Who* audition for the part of a monster—and didn't get it. But he was later cast as an American tourist, and after that was offered the part of Steven, a headstrong young man with a mind of his own.

Peter Purves eventually left *Doctor Who* because he felt that Steven wasn't getting enough of the action. But he soon got all the action he wanted on the BBC's *Blue Peter*, where he became a familiar figure to millions of children.

Anneke Wills played Polly. She started acting when she was eleven, so she had quite a lot of experience on stage, on TV and in films by the time she was offered the part. She had already had a family connection with the series. Her husband, the actor Michael Gough, had appeared on *Doctor Who*, and because she knew how much he'd enjoyed it, she had no hesitation in joining the programme. Later the family connection grew even stronger when her own children became caught up in the series, although they were rather upset by an episode which ended with her being carried off by monsters. 'They were very worried about whether I was going to come home that night!'

Michel Craze played Ben the cockney sailor. He started as a boy soprano in musicals like *The King and I* and has worked in TV since he was fifteen. He made Ben a tough self-sufficient character, and says it was hard to make your mark in a show filled with scene-stealing monsters. He has vivid memories of 'walking the plank' —in the studio tank at Ealing Studios—and of meeting his future wife on the show.

Frazer Hines played Jamie, the Highlander. He says it was a lot of fun working on *Doctor Who*. He started Jamie off with a genuine Highland accent, but had to mellow it to a sort of 'TV Scots'. Wearing a kilt all the time wasn't without its problems. 'People wanted to know, did I or didn't I wear anything under it. Well, I did—usually football shorts so I could get a game as soon as I'd finished on the set!'

Deborah Watling played Victoria. She comes from a show-business family, and her father Jack Watling once appeared on the show with her. 'Frazer and I were running downhill, away from the Yeti, when my dad, playing a professor, met us. Frazer and I charged down the mountainside to be confronted with this incredible figure with a grey beard and white hair. I couldn't believe it was Dad, and just stood there till the three of us collapsed in giggles!'

Wendy Padbury played Zoe, the Computer Operator. Although in her mid-twenties, Wendy is so small and looks so young that she can still be cast as a schoolgirl. She has very happy memories of working with Patrick Troughton and Frazer Hines. 'The three of us all left together—what a sad day.' Less happy memories include days spent filming *The War Games* in Brighton. 'We all thought we were set for a few peaceful days at the seaside, but ended by filming on Brighton rubbish tip in the freezing cold—with rats as unwelcome extras.'

Caroline John played Liz Shaw, the Scientist. Until

joining *Doctor Who* she had worked mainly in classical theatre, with the National Theatre Company, and with repertory companies all round the country. She joined the show at the same time as Jon Pertwee. 'It was a super chance. *Doctor Who* is a fabulous TV training ground, because there are so many facets to the programme. It's technically exacting, and it gave me nine months to a year of solid TV, which was a rare opportunity for a TV beginner.'

Katy Manning played Jo Grant. She says she played Jo Grant pretty much like herself—short-sighted and screaming! None of the monsters really frightened her because she couldn't see what was happening! But her near-sightedness had its problems. On her first day's filming she ran straight into a rock and tore the ligaments in her leg. But she has happier memories of her last show. Her real life fiancé Stewart Bevan played the young Professor Jones, her boyfriend in the serial.

10

The Adventures of Doctor Who

*A complete chronological summary
of the Doctor Who adventures!*

1963/4
AN UNEARTHLY CHILD (4 Episodes)
by Anthony Coburn

Susan Foreman, 15, is the Doctor's grand-daughter and
goes to Coal Hill School, London. Two teachers, Ian
Chesterton and Barbara Wright, go to investigate her
home background. 'Home' is a Police Box which is in
fact a TARDIS (standing for Time And Relative
Dimensions In Space), the Doctor's dimensionally transcendental spaceship. The old Doctor plunges them all
back to the Earth of 100,000 BC—and capture by a skin-
clad tribe which has lost the secret of fire. Two leaders,
Kal and Za, are in a power struggle. The Doctor shows
Za how to make fire, by rubbing two sticks together. Za
wants them to stay, but by a ruse they escape to the
TARDIS.

THE DEAD PLANET (7 Episodes)
by Terry Nation

On the planet Skaro live the blond Thals and the
Daleks, both survivors from a neutronic war. After
generations of mutation the Thals have become perfect
human beings. The Daleks, who lost the use of arms,
legs and bodies, are an evil intelligence housed in a
protective metal casing. A Thal tells Susan that his race
is starving. She asks the Daleks to help. But they set a

trap and the Thal leader Temmosus is killed. In a counter-attack the Daleks—powered by static electricity from their city floors—are beaten by cutting off the current, leaving them immobile.

See *Doctor Who and the Daleks.**

THE EDGE OF DESTRUCTION (2 Episodes)
by David Whitaker

In a desperate attempt to gain control of the TARDIS's guidance system and return the two school-teachers to London, 1963, the Doctor decides to experiment with a new combination. There is a violent explosion and the TARDIS stops, the doors swing open and they see they are suspended in Space, Susan and Barbara are convinced this is the mischief of an invisible alien fifth force, but Ian rationalises it as a technical fault. The irascible Doctor accuses the teachers of sabotage—with the intent of blackmailing him into returning them to Earth. Finally even Susan begins to suspect Ian and Barbara and tries to attack Ian with a pair of scissors—she is quietened by her grandfather. On reassessing the situation more calmly, they realise the halt has been caused by the ship's defence mechanism. The Doctor reluctantly admits he could have mis-set the controls. The TARDIS has only just avoided plunging into the sun—and destruction.

MARCO POLO (7 Episodes)
by John Lucarotti

The TARDIS lands in 1289 on the plateau of the Pamir, and the travellers meet Marco Polo, a young Venetian emissary of Kublai Khan's, who is on his way

* In this chapter, reference is made to the Target book of the story, where one has been published.

54

to Kublai's court in Peking, accompanied by a Tartar warlord named Tegana, a peace ambassador from the rival Mogul ruler and a Chinese girl, Ping-Cho. Marco Polo forces the Doctor to join his caravan—he wants to present the TARDIS to Kublai Khan in the hope he will be allowed to return to Venice. But Tegana wants to have the TARDIS too. In his attempts to steal the ship he tries to poison their water, and drills holes in their water barrels as they cross the Gobi desert, before escaping on the last horse. Because of the intense night cold, condensation forms on the TARDIS, so they survive. The party arrives in Peking, the Doctor meets Kublai and they play backgammon. At first the Doctor wins 35 elephants, 4,000 horses and 25 tigers. Then the tide turns and he gambles away the TARDIS. But when he exposes Tegana and saves Kublai's life, the TARDIS's key is returned to him.

THE KEYS OF MARINUS (6 Episodes)
by Terry Nation

The travellers land on the island of Marinus, where the sand is glass and the sea is acid. The TARDIS is captured by Arbitan, Keeper of the Conscience of Marinus, a machine that controls the island absolutely fairly. But the four keys that make it function are lost. The Doctor goes off to search for them. On their return Arbitan has been murdered and the island taken over by Yartek, leader of the alien Voords. The Doctor is forced to hand over the four hard-won keys, but one is an imitation and the machine explodes—blowing itself and the Voords to pieces.

THE AZTECS (4 Episodes) by John Lucarotti

In 1430, the TARDIS lands inside the Tomb of Yetaxa, one-time High Priestess of the Aztecs of Central Mexico. When the Doctor, Susan, Ian and Barbara leave the tomb, the door locks behind them. They meet Autloc, High Priest of Knowledge, and Tlotoxl, High Priest of Sacrifice. Autloc hails Barbara as Yetaxa's reincarnation —she is wearing the Priestess's bracelet, which she found in the tomb. Barbara is exalted and placed on the throne; Ian is appointed chief of the Aztec warriors, finding himself in competition with the Chosen Leader, Ixta. Ian defeats him, Ixta plunging from a pyramid to his death. Susan is made a handmaiden, but she causes a rumpus when she refuses the last wish of The Perfect Victim—marriage. The Doctor rests in luxury with the esteemed elders and, although this is incongruous to his nature, flirts mildly with a beautiful elderly Aztec lady, Cameca. This, however, is partly to learn from her a way into the tomb to retrieve the TARDIS. Barbara is declared bogus after she petitions against human sacrifices, but the crew escape—the Doctor opens the tomb door with an old-fashioned wheel-and-pulley.

THE SENSORITES (6 Episodes) by Peter R. Newman

The TARDIS lands on the deck of a gigantic spaceship from 28th-century Earth. Its Captain Maitland explains they are under the control of a race called the Sensorites, who live on Sense–Sphere planet. They are all physically identical, with huge, bald, bulb-shaped heads. Through telepathic communication with Susan, the Sensorites invite them to Sense–Sphere for talks. They explain they know the spaceship has discovered metal molybdenum on Sense–Sphere, and they are wary of being exploited. The Sensorites fear humans, for since a previous spaceship left, many of them have died. The Doctor discovers deadly nightshade in the city's water reservoirs and tracks down the culprits to underground caves—three deranged spacemen left behind from the previous expedition.

THE FRENCH REVOLUTION (6 Episodes)
by Dennis Spooner

The TARDIS lands in a forest clearing. The travellers think it's England 1963, but they are 20 kilometres from Paris during Robespierre's Reign of Terror. A farmhouse is sacked by Government troops; the Doctor is concussed and left for dead, the others dragged off to prison. The Doctor gets everyone involved in a counter-revolutionary plot by an English spy disguised as an official, who is planning Robespierre's downfall.

PLANET OF GIANTS (3 Episodes)
by Louis Marks

The doors of the TARDIS open. All readings indicate complete normality—but the time-travellers are only one inch tall! A crooked manufacturer, Forester, intends to capitalise on a new insecticide, DN6, which aims to increase food production for starving nations. He realises, however, that eventually the product will destroy every living thing, for its molecules are stable instead of ephemeral. A Government Inspector, Farrow, discovers this but is murdered by Forester before he can reveal the plot. This deed is witnessed by the miniaturised Ian and Barbara. The Doctor, against almost insurmountable odds—they are vulnerable to such hazards as being washed down plug holes and tumbling into matchboxes—stops Forester from publishing his bogus report, using a gas jet and match to cause an explosion—that goes off in the evil Forester's face.

DALEK INVASION OF EARTH (6 Episodes) by Terry Nation

London in 2164—and the Daleks have invaded Earth, making many thousands of inhabitants into Robomen— human Dalek servants—by clamping metal control discs to their heads. Other slavemen have been shipped to Bedfordshire, where the Daleks have a vast mining complex : they have discovered a fissure in the Earth's inner shell, through which they aim to remove the planet's core and replace it with a magnetic power system, so they can pilot Earth anywhere in the Universe. The Doctor and Ian are captured by Robomen and taken to the Dalek Supreme, who tries to change the Doctor into a Roboman, strapping him to an operating table in the Robotiser Chamber of a flying saucer parked in Trafalgar Square. The rest of the TARDIS crew escape from London and head for the mining fields, where Ian faces the lusts of the Slyther—the Dalek's man-eating pet. Susan and a freedom fighter named David Campbell manage to gain entry and destroy the Dalek's radio network with a bomb—created by the scientist Dortmun. This feat immobilises the Daleks' control and the Doctor orders the Robomen and the slaves to rise against the Daleks. Earth is preserved—and Susan, deeply in love, stays behind with her new boyfriend, David Campbell.

1965
THE RESCUE (2 Episodes) by David Whitaker

The Doctor lands on the planet Dido in the year 2493.

Exploring, he finds a crashed spaceship from Earth with two survivors—a paralysed man named Bennett and a young girl, Vicki. Bennett tells the Doctor the rest of the crew has been murdered by the locals, and Vicki says a native named Koquillion is protecting them from the further wrath of the enraged Didonians. The Doctor is suspicious of these explanations and challenges Koquillion—to find he is Bennett in disguise. Bennett confesses he murdered all the spaceship crew and the friendly Didonians, to conceal a murder he had previously committed on the spaceship. He had planned to take Vicki—she is oblivious of his crime—back to Earth to witness his innocence. However, two Didonian survivors terrify Bennett into plunging over a cliff to his death. The Doctor offers Vicki a chance to join his crew and she accepts.

THE ROMANS (4 Episodes) by Dennis Spooner

The TARDIS crew have been resting up in a villa outside Rome in the year AD 64, while its owner campaigns in the Gallic wars. When Vicki and the Doctor visit Rome, Barbara and Ian are captured by slave-traders—Ian is sold as a galley slave and Barbara to the court of Nero. The Doctor is mistaken for Maximus Pettulian, celebrated musician and enemy of Nero, and is taken to the Emperor's Palace (the Doctor cannot play a note of music). Ian escapes from the galley ship, only to be sent to Rome as a gladiator, where he encounters Barbara. With his spectacle lens the Doctor sets fire to the plans Nero has rejected for his 'perfect city'—inspiring Nero for the Great Fire of Rome, under cover of which the crew of the TARDIS escape back to the villa.

THE WEB PLANET (6 Episodes)
by Bill Strutton

The TARDIS is drawn by an unknown force to the planet Vortis. While the Doctor and Ian explore, the force causes Barbara to leave the TARDIS. Eventually the ant-like Zarbi take her, and three of the butterfly-like Menoptra, to a slave colony. The Zarbi drag the TARDIS to their Web headquarters. The Doctor and Ian follow the tracks and the Doctor talks to the unseen force, the Animus, about an invasion by the Menoptra to regain their planet. The invasion is a failure, but the Doctor manages to obtain a cell-destructor brought to Vortis during the invasion. The Doctor and Vicki are taken to the Animus where Ian and Barbara arrive. Barbara uses the cell-destructor and the Animus is destroyed.

See *Doctor Who and the Zarbi*.

THE CRUSADERS (4 Episodes)
by David Whitaker

Twelfth-century Palestine: Saracens, led by a Saladin emir, El Akir, wait to ambush Richard the Lionheart. The Doctor gets involved. Richard plans for peace by arranging a marriage between Saladin's brother Saphadin and his own sister, Joanna. But Joanna refuses. The Doctor and Vicki narrowly escape being burnt at the stake.

See *Doctor Who and the Crusaders*.

THE SPACE MUSEUM (4 Episodes)
by Glyn Jones

The white dust planet of Xeros has been made into a Space Museum, devoted to the display of the warlike

Morok Empire's historical conquests—including familiar enemies like the Daleks. The Doctor—who has become invisible—sees their own replicas in the museum, and realises the TARDIS has jumped ahead in time and to avoid ending up as exhibits they must change this future. They learn of a revolution by the Xerons, in which the Doctor helps them to victory.

THE CHASE (6 Episodes) by Terry Nation

The Daleks follow the TARDIS to exterminate the Doctor, for his interference with their plans. After a brief encounter on the desert planet Aridus, the TARDIS lands on the Empire State Building, the Mary Celeste, a gothic castle with Dracula and Frankenstein's monster, and finally on the Mechanoid planet, Mechanus. There the travellers are taken prisoner and meet the only human on the planet, Steven Taylor, the survivor of a spaceship crash. The Daleks and Mechanoids fight and destroy each other, leaving the Dalek time machine. Ian and Barbara use this to get back to their own time. Steven stays with the Doctor.

THE TIME MEDDLER (4 Episodes)
by Dennis Spooner

TARDIS materialises on the rocky east coast of England in 1066. There they are puzzled to find a modern wristwatch and a tape-recorder. Their owner, the Monk, is another time-traveller, now planning to ensure Harold wins the Battle of Hastings with atomic bazookas. It takes all the Doctor's ingenuity to upset the Meddling Monk's plans. Finally he removes the Monk's dimension controller, leaving his TARDIS stuck in 1066.

GALAXY FOUR (4 Episodes)
by William Emms

A planet in Galaxy Four is about to spin out of orbit, so the women-dominated Drahvins plan to escape in the spaceship of the planet's other inhabitants, the Rills. The Doctor lends power from the TARDIS for the ship of the gentle humane Rills to escape destruction.

MISSION TO THE UNKNOWN (1 Episode)
by Terry Nation

The setting is the planet Kembel, whence information of mysterious happenings has reached the Space Special Security Service. Agent Marc Cory is despatched there to investigate, but almost at once disaster strikes: his crew are cut down one by one by the alien horrors which infest the planet. But what Cory discovers is of vital importance for the future of Earth: the Daleks, controlled as ever by the Dalek Supreme, are present in force on Kembel and their intention is to attempt once more the destruction of their dedicated opponents: the humanoids.

THE MYTH MAKERS (4 Episodes)
by Donald Cotton

On the plains outside a besieged Troy, the Doctor is hailed as Zeus and taken by Achilles to his camp. But a fellow-warrior, Odysseus, is sceptical as to his authenticity and gives him two days to devise a plan to capture Troy. Meanwhile the TARDIS is seized by a Trojan prince and Vicki is hailed as a prophetess. She and Steven are thrown into jail and Vicki is given two days to prove her supernatural powers. At the Greek camp the Doctor decides his attack on Troy will be with a huge wooden horse. They wheel it into the city and the Greeks emerge from inside the horse, open the gates and take the city. Vicki elects to remain behind with the fleeing Trojans.

1965/66
THE DALEK MASTER PLAN (12 Episodes)
by Terry Nation & Dennis Spooner

The Doctor lands on the planet Kembel in 4000 AD, where the space security agent Bret Vyon is trying to warn that the Daleks are about to destroy Earth. Bret is shot, being mistaken for a traitor. The TARDIS lands on the volcanic planet Tigus to be pursued by the Meddling Monk (see 'The Time Meddler'). Finally on Kembel, the Doctor activates the time destructor, wiping out the Dalek invasion—but killing space agent Sarah Kingdom.

THE MASSACRE (4 Episodes)
by John Lucarotti

It is Paris before the Eve of St Bartholomew's, 1572, and the Catholic Queen Mother Catherine de Medici is planning to massacre all French Protestants. The Doctor and Steven arrive and Steven meets some Huguenots from the Protestant Admiral de Coligny's household. They rescue a servant girl, Anne, who has overheard the planning of the massacre plot, but the Admiral does not believe her. Later the Catholic Abbot of Amboise arrives at the Admiral's house. He is the Doctor's double. Steven believes he *is* the Doctor and follows him and overhears the plan to assassinate de Coligny. The attempt fails. The Catholic undercover leader, Marshal Tavannes, blames the Abbot for this failure and orders his execution. The Doctor and his companions escape Paris as the massacre begins.

THE ARK (4 Episodes)
by Paul Erickson & Lesley Scott

The Earth is about to plunge into the Sun. The Human race, miniaturised, and all Earth life is in a huge Ark on a 700 year voyage to a new planet, Refusis. Dodo has a cold which Steven, the human guardians of the Ark and the slave race called the Monoids have no immunity to. The Doctor eventually finds a cure and takes off, but the TARDIS only goes seven hundred years into the future, to the end of the Ark's voyage. The cold returned and made the Monoids strong and the Guardians their slaves. With the help of the invisible Refusians, the Doctor forces the Monoids and Humans to make peace and live together on Refusis.

THE CELESTIAL TOYMAKER (4 Episodes)
by Brian Hayles

TARDIS materialises in the domain of the Celestial Toymaker, an evil force who dominates a fantasy world. He is a happy-looking mandarin character dressed in a splendid bejewelled coat. He invites the Doctor to be his partner in the complex Trilogic Game. Steven and Dodo are set a series of puzzles and games, which if they lose will render them subjects of the Toymaker. Their first opponents are the clowns Joey and Clara, with whom they play Blind Man's Buff—and win. Then they meet the Hearts family and play a macabre game of musical chairs. After that they find themselves trying to reach the end of a ballroom dodging dancing dolls. Their fourth—and most lethal—opponent is the ob-

64

noxious schoolboy, Cyril. With him they play a death-trap dice game across electrified triangles—but manage to reach 'home' first. The Doctor triumphs over the Toymaker by imitating the magician's voice—and the travellers are on their way once again.

THE GUNFIGHTERS (4 Episodes)
by Donald Cotton

The Doctor, Steven and Dodo arrive in Tombstone on 26 October 1881. The Doctor has toothache and finds the local dentist is none other than the infamous Doc Holliday, who is feuding with the Clanton family. The Clantons' gunfighter, 'Snake-eyes' Harper, nearly guns down the Doctor by mistake. Marshal Wyatt Earp arrests the Doctor and rescues Steven from lynching. Pa Clanton hires gunfighter Johnny Ringo, and on to the famous shoot-out, Earp winning—at the OK Corral.

THE SAVAGES (4 Episodes)
by Ian Stuart Black

On a distant planet live the ultra-civilised Elders and the wild primitive Savages. The TARDIS crew are escorted to the Elders' capital to meet their leader, Jano. Steven and Dodo are taken on a conducted tour of the city, and inevitably the curious Dodo takes a detour—and finds herself in a strange laboratory presided over by Senta. When Dodo is back with the Doctor the truth suddenly dawns: this 'advanced civilisation' has been formed by transferring the life force and energy of the Savages into the Elders. The Doctor protests, but for his pains his own life force is transferred to Jano. This means that Jano adopts some of the Doctor's attitudes—and con-science. With this new perspective, Jano goes out into the Savages' wilderness and recruits them to destroy the transference laboratory The Elders and Savages choose Steven to be their leader, so Dodo and the Doctor leave him there to his task.

THE WAR MACHINES (4 Episodes)
by Ian Stuart Black

The TARDIS has materialised outside London's Post Office Tower. Inside it they find Professor Brett and his revolutionary computer called WOTAN—Will Operating Thought Analogue—a universal problem-solver that can think for itself. Suddenly the machine reverses its process and starts to take over men, beginning with Brett. WOTAN programmes them to build War Machines—self-contained mobile computers—to prepare for the invasion of mankind. Ben, a young merchant seaman who has befriended Dodo, and Brett's secretary Polly are captured, but Ben escapes and warns top civil servant Sir Charles Summer. Troops are powerless against War Machines, but by using a series of field forces the Doctor re-programmes one to destroy WOTAN. Dodo decides to stay in England.

THE SMUGGLERS (4 Episodes)
by Brian Hayles

Ben and Polly's adventures on a wild remote part of 17th-century Cornish coast. Pirates are searching for treasure, while smugglers (who include the local Squire) are trying to sell contraband. The Doctor unwittingly receives a clue to the treasure's whereabouts from the Churchwarden—just before a pirate murders him. The pirates try to extract the information from the Doctor. The TARDIS's crew are rescued by the militia.

THE TENTH PLANET (4 Episodes)
by Kit Pedler and Gerry Davis

In the late 1980s the TARDIS lands at a South Pole Space Tracking Station, where General Cutler battles with invaders from the Tenth Planet, Mondas— Earth's missing half. Mondas is draining away the energy of Earth. The planet's inhabitants appear: ruthless silver-clad figures called Cybermen, whose original bodies have been replaced with plastic to make them disease-free and invulnerable. The Cybermen take control of Earth, and at the South Pole Base they plan to use the powerful Z-bomb to destroy Earth before Mondas is itself destroyed, and at the same time take Earth people to Mondas to become Cybermen. Ben outwits them, and before the Cybermen can again infiltrate the Base, Mondas absorbs too much energy and is destroyed. Without energy from Mondas the Cybermen die. Worn out by the strain of recent events the Doctor seems to grow very old and when he returns to the TARDIS he begins to change ...

See *Doctor Who and the Tenth Planet*.

THE POWER OF THE DALEKS (6 Episodes)
by David Whitaker

A fully recovered Doctor has been rejuvenated and has a totally new appearance and personality. TARDIS materialises on the Earth colony Vulcan in 2020. In a space rocket from the Mercury Swamp the Doctor finds two inanimate Daleks. But Lesterson, the Chief Scientist, has removed one, reactivated it, and plans to use Daleks as servants. Rebels out to overthrow the colony's Governor decide to use the reactivated Daleks to help them. The Daleks have secretly set up a reproduction plant—on a conveyor-belt system—and plan to 'exterminate all humans'. But the Doctor finds their power source and turns it against them.

1966/7
THE HIGHLANDERS (4 Episodes)
by Elwyn Jones & Gerry Davis

TARDIS lands on a Scottish moor in 1746 near the battlefield of Culloden, which has just seen the English defeat of the Scots and Bonnie Prince Charlie. The Doctor and his friends come across a group of hunted Highlanders led by clan laird Colin McLaren and accompanied by his daughter Kirsty and faithful piper Jamie. The Highlanders and time-travellers are captured by English Lieutenant Algernon ffinch. At the English camp a crooked solicitor, Grey, is working out a scheme to transport prisoners to slavery in the West Indies. The Doctor escapes and gets arms to the Scottish prisoners, held aboard a stolen ship, the *Annabelle*. Grey and the ship's captain are overpowered and the ship returned to its owner, who takes the Scots to safety in France. The TARDIS dematerialises with an extra passenger—Jamie.

THE UNDERWATER MENACE (4 Episodes)
by Geoffrey Orme

The TARDIS lands on an extinct volcanic rock surrounded by sea. On leaving their ship the Doctor and his companions are kidnapped by the primitive Atlanteans and taken below the sea to the city of Atlantis. There its inhabitants plan to sacrifice the travellers to their goddess Amdo, suspending them over a pool of hungry sharks. They are rescued by the scientist Zaroff, who has a plan to destroy the world by draining the ocean into the white hot core of Earth so the super-heated steam will explode it in two. Zaroff takes the Doctor with him, sends Ben and Jamie to the mines and orders that Polly undergo an operation to become a fish worker, collecting food from the sea. The TARDIS crew escape and persuade the fish workers to revolt, but Zaroff is unperturbed, for he is confident that within twelve hours the world will be destroyed. He becomes the victim of his own scheme when the Doctor enters the generating plant and accelerates the fission to break down the sea walls. Zaroff is drowned by the flood waters; the others escape.

THE MOONBASE (4 Episodes)
by Kit Pedler

In the year 2070 Hobson and his deputy Benoit command a Weather Station on the Moon. There they operate the Gravitron, a gravity machine which has control over the weather on Earth. When the Doctor arrives on the Moon he finds that a mysterious disease has broken out. He investigates, and in the midst of problems, like strange kidnappings and the Gravitron losing co-ordination, discovers that the Cybermen have landed. They are responsible for the disease that has smitten the space station, and the Gravitron's peculiar behaviour. It is all part of a well-planned Cybermen plot to take 'control' of the kidnapped men and force them to operate the Gravitron, enabling the Cybermen to destroy Earth by drastically altering its weather. Polly retaliates by spraying the plastic Cybermen with fire extinguishers filled with solvents, but the main enemy force is approaching. Suddenly the Doctor realises that the Cybermen are susceptible to gravity—that is why they had to have humans working the Gravitron—so by deflecting this machine on to the Moon's surface the monsters and their ships are sent shooting off into the distant limits of outer space.

See *Doctor Who and the Cybermen*.

THE MACRA TERROR (4 Episodes)
by Ian Stuart Black

The Doctor and his friends find themselves in the distant future on a planet run like a gigantic holiday camp. A man called Medok tells the Doctor it is being infiltrated at night by crab-like creatures called Macra. The Macra are in control of this 'paradise' and have conditioned the workers to quarry the deadly gas they survive on. The Doctor takes control of the gas-pumping machine and stops the life flow to the Macra. Ben clinches the victory by blowing up the gas pumps.

THE FACELESS ONES (6 Episodes)
by David Ellis & Malcolm Hulke

It is Gatwick airport in 1966 and the TARDIS materialises on the runway in front of an incoming jet. While Polly hides in a hanger she is witness to the murder of a policeman. Then Polly and Ben are kidnapped and the Doctor discovers others have disappeared—all passengers on Chameleon Tours charter flights. The kidnappers are the Chameleons, a race from another planet who have lost their identity in a nuclear explosion and are dying out. Their scientists have devised a method for taking over the identity of humans—the transference taking four weeks. The Chameleons have got aboard aircraft and miniaturised 50,000 passengers, presently being held in a space station hundreds of miles above Earth. The Doctor succeeds in freeing them. Ben and Polly remain in the England of 1966.

THE EVIL OF THE DALEKS (7 Episodes)
by David Whitaker

The TARDIS is stolen and driven off in a lorry. The Doctor and Jamie follow it and arrive at a Victoriana antique shop owned by the ancient Edward Waterfield. All three are transported back 100 years to the home of scientist Theodore Maxtible. The Daleks are holding Waterfield's daughter Victoria prisoner—it is they who forced her father to travel through time as Maxtible to bring the Doctor back to 1867. They coerce the Doctor to run an experiment on Jamie, registering every emotion he shows while rescuing Victoria. The resulting 'human factors' are injected into three new Daleks, but it proves disastrous, as the Daleks adopt attitudes of playful friendliness instead of cunning! All are recalled to the Dalek planet of Skaro, where the Emperor Dalek tells the Doctor he is to take the Dalek 'factor' back to Earth—the impulse to destroy. The Doctor is passed through a machine transforming humans into mental Daleks, but the Doctor is unaffected, for he is not a human. Instead, he humanises the Daleks.

THE TOMB OF THE CYBERMEN (4 Episodes)
by Kit Pedler and Gerry Davis

TARDIS materialises in the future on the planet of Telos, where the time-travellers meet an Earth archaeological expedition financed by a strange couple named Kaftan and Klieg. They are evacuating the last remains of the now-extinct Cybermen. But the Cybermen are revived by a rise in temperature engineered by the deranged Klieg. Victoria saves the party from the Tombs, but the Cybermen retaliate by sending Cybermats—small metallic creatures—to attack them. The Doctor neutralises them and freezes the Cybermen to inactivity.

THE ABOMINABLE SNOWMEN (6 Episodes)
by Mervyn Haisman and Henry Lincoln

Explorer Travers is in the Himalayas searching for the Yeti when his companion is killed. Travers accuses the Doctor of his friend's murder. The Yeti are fur-covered Robots, directed by an evil Intelligence. The Doctor overcomes them, frustrating the Intelligence's plan to destroy the world.

See *Doctor Who and the Abominable Snowmen*.

THE ICE WARRIORS (6 Episodes)
by Brian Hayles

It is England during the second Ice Age. The Doctor and his companions seek refuge in a scientific base where the ice barrier is being combatted by an ioniser. Embedded in the ice face is a perfectly preserved body of what appears to be a Viking warrior. Varga, the Ice Warrior, is revived at the base, but he captures Victoria. He is in fact a Martian Captain of a spaceship which crash-landed in the ice. He is intent on freeing his craft. The Doctor takes over the base and uses the ioniser at full strength to create an explosion—melting the Martians and halting the ice flow.

See *Doctor Who and the Ice Warriors*.

1967/8
THE ENEMY OF THE WORLD (6 Episodes)
by David Whitaker

Arriving on an Australian beach the time-travellers are attacked by a hovercraft, then rescued by a helicopter girl named Astrid. Her boss, Giles Kent, explains that the Doctor is the double of a would-be world dictator, Salamander. Jamie and Victoria infiltrate Salamander's retinue and discover he is the instigator of the 'natural' disasters sweeping the world. But Jamie and Victoria are captured, and to organise their rescue the Doctor impersonates Salamander. He penetrates Salamander's office and is confronted by Kent, who is planning to seize Salamander's power. Salamander impersonates the Doctor and tries to steal the TARDIS. He is ejected into Space.

THE WEB OF FEAR (6 Episodes)
by Mervyn Haisman and Henry Lincoln

In mid-space, a cobweb-type substance envelopes the TARDIS and the time travellers find themselves on a deserted London Underground station. They meet an old friend, Professor Travers (from 'The Abominable Snowmen', 1966/67) who confesses he has constructed and reactivated a Yeti. This in its turn has brought the return of the Intelligence. Yeti are at large in the Underground; the Doctor is captured and a brain-draining helmet placed on his head. But he attempts to drain the brain from the Intelligence, and almost succeeds—until he is rescued by well-meaning friends, leaving the Intelligence free again.

See *Doctor Who and the Web of Fear*.

FURY FROM THE DEEP (6 Episodes)
by Victor Pemberton

The Doctor and his companions are suspected of sabotage at a North Sea gas refinery off the east coast of England. The refinery boss, Robson, blames them for the disappearance of rig-crews, and leaks and pressure build-ups in the pipelines. The Doctor reports strange 'heart-beats' from the pipelines, but Robson refuses to halt the gas flow. The noises come from a form of parasitic sea-weed, which absorbs human brains and transforms men

73

into weed creatures. The weed launches an attack on the refinery, but after Victoria's screaming kills one the Doctor discovers that the creatures can be destroyed by high-frequency sound waves. Victoria decides to remain at the refinery.

THE WHEEL IN SPACE (6 Episodes)
by David Whitaker

Inside a drifting rocket lurks a hostile Servo Robot. The rocket is in the orbit of a space station called 'The Wheel', where there have been reports of 'space rodents'. These are Cybermats, creations of the Cybermen, who are planning an Earth invasion. The Doctor annihilates the Cybermen's invasion fleet and travels on with Jamie and a new companion, Zoe.

THE DOMINATORS (5 Episodes)
by Norman Ashby

TARDIS materialises on the planet of Dulkis, now taken over by the alien Dominators and their robot servants the Quarks. The Dulcians are pacifists and cannot retaliate. They ignore the Doctor's warnings and some of them are captured. The Doctor discovers the Dominators' plan; to fire rockets down bore holes, causing an eruption of the molten core of the planet. They will then drop an atomic seed capsule down a bore-hole, turning Dulkis into a radio-active mass, fuel for the Dominator space fleet. Jamie and Cully, rebellious son of the Dulcian leader, become impatient and destroy a Quark, and the Doctor and Zoe are captured by Dominators. The Doctor intercepts the seed capsule as it is dropped, and conceals it in the Dominator ship, destroying it in an atomic blast.

THE MIND ROBBER (5 Episodes)
by Peter Ling

The TARDIS arrives in the Land of Fiction, a huge white void where fiction appears as reality. The travellers are hunted by White Robots and encounter mechanical soldiers. Jamie gains entry to the Citadel of the Master, an aged gentleman who wants to retire from rule and insists the Doctor takes his place. The Doctor refuses, so the White Robots capture Jamie and Zoe. In the following battle of wits the Doctor calls up champions from fiction to defeat the Master, and the time travellers escape.

THE INVASION (8 Episodes)
by Derrick Sherwin

The Doctor calls at the home of his friend Professor Travers, but finds he has let it to a computer scientist, Professor Watkins, and his niece Isobel. Watkins has disappeared—last heard of at International Electromatics, a firm controlling all the world's computers. The Doctor visits the firm and distrusts its managing director, Tobias Vaughn. So does Brigadier Lethbridge-Stewart of UNIT (United Nations Intelligence Taskforce). Zoe and Isobel are captured by Vaughn, forcing Watkins to develop the Cerebration Mentor. The Doctor discovers Vaughn is in the power of the Cybermen, who launch an invasion through the sewers and paralyse Earth's population. A reformed Vaughn helps the Doctor destroy the Cybermen's spaceship.

THE KROTONS (4 Episodes)
by Robert Holmes

The primitive Gonds are ruled and taught through the Machine of the Krotons. The Krotons are monsters waiting in suspended animation until they have drained enough mental energy from the Gonds' brains to be re-animated. Each year the two most brilliant Gonds are lured into the Kroton Machine. Zoe and the Doctor take the Teaching Machine Test and their mental power reanimates the Krotons. The Doctor discovers the Kroton life system is based on telurium. He destroys them with acid.

THE SEEDS OF DEATH (6 Episodes)
by Brian Hayles

Earth in the 21st century enjoys the T-Mat, a form of instantaneous travel directed from a Moon relay station. The machine breaks and the Doctor investigates. He finds the Moon overrun by Ice Warriors, who are preparing to launch an invasion against Earth. To weaken Earth's resistance they are using the T-Mat to send Martian Seed Pods, emitting a lethal fungus, over Earth's winter zones. The Doctor manages to get himself and the T-Mat back to a now chaotic Earth, where Ice Warriors have taken over control of the weather. The only things that can combat the fungus are water and warmth. The Doctor destroys it with torrential rain.

THE SPACE PIRATES (6 Episodes)
by Robert Holmes

The TARDIS materialises on a navigation beacon far out in Space. One of these has been stolen and the International Space Corps is convinced the thief is an inno-

cent yet eccentric space mining pioneer named Milo
Clancey. Milo joins forces with the Doctor, and the
TARDIS crew hide him on the planet of Ta. Here
dwells Caven, a notorious space criminal in league with
space pirates. Caven is assisted by Madeleine, daughter
of his ex-partner, Dom Issigri—who is Caven's captive.
Madeleine sees the error of her ways.

THE WAR GAMES (10 Episodes)
by Terrance Dicks and Malcolm Hulke

The TARDIS materialises in what appears to be no
man's land on a First World War battlefront in France.
The crew escape and when they emerge from a cloud
of mist find that they are really on another planet. It is
split into zones and in each a fierce war is being waged.
The wars are controlled by the Aliens, who have
gathered soldiers from many periods of history, brain-
washed them and put them to battle. The aim : to form
an invincible army from the survivors and take over the
Galaxy. The Doctor seizes the Alien HQ and calls on
the Time Lords for help. His masters capture him, find
him guilty of stealing the TARDIS and exile him to
Earth.

1970
SPEARHEAD FROM SPACE (4 Episodes)
by Robert Holmes

Fifty meteorites fall, and the Brigadier and his newly
recruited scientist Liz Shaw, from Cambridge, enlist the
aid of a physically changed Doctor. Factory boss Chan-
ning is a Nestene—they colonise planets by copying the
native life forms—and is making plastic fighting Autons,
as well as plastic facsimiles of the Cabinet to gain world

domination. The Doctor defeats them, and agrees to work for UNIT in return for facilities to repair his TARDIS. The Brigadier gives him a sprightly yellow roadster, Bessie.

THE SILURIANS (7 Episodes)
by Malcolm Hulke

On Wenley Moor, a secret Derbyshire atomic research centre where a reactor converting nuclear energy to electrical power is being developed, work is being held up by inexplicable power losses and breakdowns among staff. The Doctor traces the trouble to underground caves where prehistoric monsters live with a nest of highly intelligent man-like reptiles, the Silurians. They went into hibernation millions of years ago, but have been resuscitated by accidental electrical discharges from the research centre and now claim back 'their' Earth. The Doctor strives for harmony between Man and Silurian, and at first seems to succeed with the Old Silurian. But then the rebellious and intolerant Young Silurian releases a terrible disease that will wipe out man. The Doctor finds an antidote. The Silurians take over the centre and plan to destroy the Van Allen Belt, which shields Earth from the sun. The reptiles are tricked into returning to their caves by threat of radiation and the Brigadier—to the Doctor's disgust—blows them up.

See *Doctor Who and the Cave Monsters*.

THE AMBASSADORS OF DEATH (7 Episodes)
by David Whitaker

Seven months after leaving Mars, the 'Probe Seven' ship has still not returned to Earth, and a 'Recovery Seven' rocket is despatched to investigate. Contact is made, but the sound Space Control Centre receives is a scrambled signal, which is replied to from an abandoned London warehouse. 'Recovery Seven' returns to Earth, but after landing the astronauts are kidnapped by men masquerading as UNIT forces. Then Liz Shaw notices the ship's Geiger counter is at maximum, which would have killed the crew by radiation. The Doctor is convinced they are not human. He makes a solo space mission and finds the real astronauts held aboard a large alien spaceship.

INFERNO (7 Episodes) by Don Houghton

Crisis at a top secret drilling project—Inferno—which aims to penetrate the Earth's crust and release a new energy source to be called Stahlman's Gas. The drilling pipes are leaking a liquid which turns green on contact with the skin and transforms its victims into Primords—vicious primeval apes. The Doctor transports himself into a parallel world, where the Inferno Project is about to destroy the planet. On his return to 'our' world he manages to thwart the power-crazed Professor Stahlman, who has now become a full Primord.

TERROR OF THE AUTONS (4 Episodes) by Robert Holmes

Introducing the Master, who materialises in a horsebox at Rossini's Circus. Another Time Lord warns the Doctor and his new assistant Jo Grant, who realise that with the Master's help the Nestenes are planning a new invasion using the Autons. In a battle between Autons and UNIT forces, the Master, to save his own life, helps the Doctor—then escapes, to fight another day.

See *Doctor Who and the Terror of the Autons*.

THE MIND OF EVIL (6 Episodes)
by Don Houghton

The Doctor suspects an alien mind parasite in the Keller machine, which extracts evil from criminals' minds; in London the Chinese delegate dies at the World Peace Conference; and a UNIT officer is in charge of dumping a banned Thunderbolt nerve gas missile at sea. Professor Keller is really the Master, who captures the Doctor and Jo by inciting a riot at Stangmoor Prison. He incites the convicts to hi-jack the nerve gas missile to destroy the peace conference. The Doctor traps the Master, by using the mind parasite, then explodes it with the nerve gas.

CLAWS OF AXOS (4 Episodes)
by Dave Martin and Bob Baker

An alien spaceship contains the Axons: humanoid, friendly, beautiful. They ask for hospitality on Earth to regenerate, as their planet has been crippled by a solar flare. A suspicious Doctor discovers that the Axons, their ship and a material called Axonite are all part of a parasite brought by the Master to absorb all living energy on Earth. The Doctor forces Axos into a 'time loop', destroying the Axons.

COLONY IN SPACE (6 Episodes)
by Malcolm Hulke

The Time Lords permit the TARDIS to make its first voyage through time and space for more than a year. For the Master has stolen the Doomsday Machine file, and it must be retrieved. The Time Lords despatch the Doctor and Jo to a bleak Earth-type planet in the year 2471, where they meet the Colonists, farmers who left

Sarah Jane Smith (Elisabeth Sladen) being held hostage by the Giant Robot.
A scene from 'Dr Who and the Robot'.

The Doctor, in each of his four very different incarnations. *Above left* as played by William Hartnell, the first Doctor and described as 'a crotchety old man'; *Above right* Patrick Troughton, 'a sort of cosmic hobo'; *Below* Jon Pertwee, who as third Doctor brought a dash of style to the role, seen here fighting off a pterodactyl; and *Opposite* Tom Baker, the current Doctor, a happy mixture of hero and buffoon, clown and genius.

Above The Doctor (Tom Baker) makes a brave attempt to stop the advance of the monster Morbius. A scene from 'Dr Who and the Brain of Morbius'. *Below* The unexpected arrival of a Cyberman.

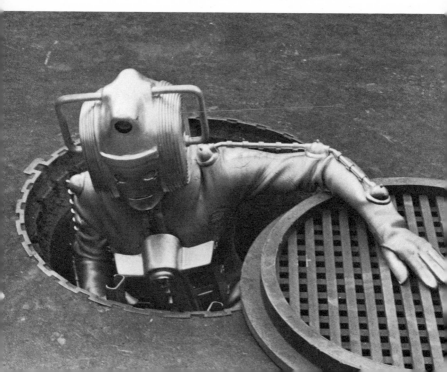

Above left Davros, fanatical creator of the dreaded Daleks. A scene from 'Dr Who and the Genesis of the Daleks'. *Above right* The Doctor (Tom Baker) finds himself surrounded by an army of Daleks. *Below* The Doctor (Tom Baker) and Sarah (Elisabeth Sladen) move cautiously among the Egyptian relics. A scene from 'Dr Who and the Pyramids of Mars'.

Not just an ordinary London Police Box, this is the TARDIS, about to transport the Doctor (Tom Baker) and Sarah (Elisabeth Sladen) off on yet another adventure.

Above The first three Doctors get together. *Below* Tom Baker and an enthusiastic crowd at one of his very popular book-signing sessions.

Above What is this strange monster doing in an English country garden? *Below* It's getting a bit too close for comfort! Sarah Jane Smith (Elisabeth Sladen) takes protection behind the Doctor (Tom Baker). Scenes from 'Dr Who and the Seeds of Doom'.

Earth because of overcrowding. Since their arrival they have faced inexplicable crop failures. There are two other groups on the planet: the Primitives, its original savage inhabitants, who steal the TARDIS and imprison Jo in their underground city, and Earthmen from the Interplanetary Mining Corporation, who have come to exploit the rich mineral deposits. If successful, they would make the planet uninhabitable. The IMC have been demoralising the Colonists with attacks by robot lizards. An adjudicator from Earth, brought in to judge between the relative merits of mining and farming, is impersonated by the Master, whose aim is to regain the stolen Doomsday Machine from a nearby ruined city, where it is maintained by non-human alien priests. The Doctor and Jo struggle to prevent the exile of the Colonists and to stop the Master from seizing the Machine. The Guardian, sole survivor of the race that built the Machine, helps the Doctor to set it to self destruct.

See *Doctor Who and the Doomsday Weapon*.

THE DAEMONS (5 Episodes)
by Guy Leopold

Against the advice of a local white witch, a prehistoric barrow at Devil's End is cut open. A mysterious force erupts, killing the professor responsible for the excavation, and concussing the Doctor. When he recovers he finds the village cut off by a heat barrier. The Master—posing as the new vicar—has used psionic science to release the power of a Daemon named Azal. The Doctor shows the Brigadier how to make a 'tunnel' through the heat barrier. Azal offers his power to the Doctor. The Doctor declines, and is about to be destroyed for his rejection when Jo presents herself as a substitute. Azal is so confused by such irrationality that he kills himself. The Master is finally captured and imprisoned.

See *Doctor Who and the Daemons*.

1972
THE DAY OF THE DALEKS (4 Episodes)
by Louis Marks

The peace diplomat Sir Reginald Styles is attacked by guerrillas, who escape to their 22nd-century world, taking the Doctor with them. They are ruled by the Daleks and their ape-like slaves, the Ogrons. The guerrillas say they are after Styles because in the 20th century he murdered world leaders, making them vulnerable to Dalek attacks. They want to prevent this. The Doctor realises the real murderer was a guerrilla still in Styles' house. He hurries to the present and evacuates the house. The guerrilla Shura destroys the Daleks with a Dalakanium bomb.

See *Doctor Who and the Day of the Daleks*.

THE CURSE OF PELADON (4 Episodes)
by Brian Hayles

The primitive planet of Peladon has applied for membership of the Galactic Federation. King Peladon and Chancellor Torbis favour the union; High Priest Hepesh does not. Torbis is murdered and Aggedor, a semi-mythical monster, is blamed. The Doctor arrives, and is taken for the Earth's delegate. Hepesh captures the King and orders Aggedor to kill him. But the Doctor has tamed the monster.

See *Doctor Who and the Curse of Peladon*.

THE SEA DEVILS (6 Episodes)
by Malcolm Hulke

The Doctor and Jo visit the Master, in exile on a small island. The Governor, Colonel Trenchard, tells them that ships have been mysteriously disappearing. They investigate and the Doctor is attacked by an underwater Silurian, a man-like lizard known as a Sea Devil. The Doctor discovers that the Master, assisted by a misguided Trenchard, is stealing electrical equipment from a naval base to build a machine that will control the Sea Devils—and then conquer the world. The Doctor enters the Sea Devils' base and tries to encourage peace. But his efforts are frustrated by a depth charge attack ordered by a ruthless politician, Walker. The Doctor persuades Walker to allow him a final attempt at peace, but in the meantime the Sea Devils capture the naval base. The evil Master then forces the Doctor to help finish his machine, which will revive Sea Devil colonies all over the world. The Sea Devils' scheme is to kill the Master, whose use to them would be over. But the Doctor sabotages the machine and escapes with the Master—to see the monsters blow up. The Master escapes once more in a stolen hovercraft.

See *Doctor Who and the Sea Devils*.

THE MUTANTS (6 Episodes)
by Bob Baker and Dave Martin

The planet Solos is to become independent, to the chagrin of its Marshal. He commissions a Solonian to murder the Earth administrator, and plans to oxygenise the Solonian atmosphere. Ky, a Solonian, is unjustly accused of the murder. On Solos, Doctor Who meets Sondergaard, who is searching for a cure for the mutating disease which threatens the Solonians. The Doctor is forced to perfect the Marshall's oxygenising machine, but Sondergaard gives Ky a crystal which turns him first into a Mutant, then into a super-being. Ky kills the Marshal and takes the crystal, which will help the rest of the Solonians to evolve into super-beings too.

THE TIME MONSTER (6 Episodes)
by Robert Sloman

Professor Thascales (the Master) is working on TOM-TIT—Transmission Of Matter Through Interstitial Time. The Doctor discovers he aims to go through time to Atlantis and steal the Crystal of Kronos. The Doctor tries to foil him, but the Master evokes the fury of Kronos, and Atlantis is destroyed.

1972/3
THE THREE DOCTORS (4 Episodes)
by Bob Baker and Dave Martin

The energy of the Time Lords is being drained by a mysterious 'black hole' in space. And a cosmic ray research balloon brings back a blob of animated grey gell which dematerialises people on contact. It expands and besieges the Doctor and Jo in the TARDIS. The only way the Time Lords can help is by sending the Doctor's previous selves ... The brains of the three Doctors discover the incidents are caused by Omega, a bitter Time Lord trapped in a universe of anti-matter for thousands of years. The three Doctors cross the time bridge and rematerialise in Omega's world of anti-matter. They destroy Omega by making him a supernova and the three Doctors return to their rightful places in time and space.

See *Doctor Who—The Three Doctors*.

84

CARNIVAL OF MONSTERS (4 Episodes)
by Robert Holmes

The TARDIS lands on a cargo ship crossing the Indian Ocean in 1926. Or does it? Doctor Who and Jo discover that not only are they on an alien planet trapped in a time loop, but they are captives of showman Vorg, his assistant Shirna and their Scope—a miniaturised peepshow of Galaxy life forms. The Doctor tries to escape by entering another section of the Scope—a swamp—where he is confronted by the Drashigs, huge underwater dragons. Finally the Doctor breaks out of the Scope and materialises to full size. He becomes involved in the intrigues of two natives, Kalik and Orum, who plan to overthrow their superior, Zarb, by allowing the Drashigs to escape. Vorg destroys the Drashigs and the Doctor breaks the time link by contriving to link the TARDIS to the Scope—returning the unwilling peepshow participants to their rightful Galaxy times and places.

FRONTIER IN SPACE (6 Episodes)
by Malcolm Hulke

To avoid a head-on collision in space the Doctor and Jo materialise in the hold of a future Earth spaceship. Almost immediately the rocket is attacked. They emerge from the hold and the crew 'see' them as their enemies, the Draconians—an alien humanoid race rivalling Earth for control of the Galaxy. The Doctor and Jo, however, see the attackers as Ogrons. A rescue ship takes them all to Earth, where the Doctor is accused of being a Draconian spy. He is then captured by the Draconians and branded as an agent-provocateur in the pay of Earth. The Doctor realises there is a third party using the Ogrons to provoke war. After adventures in deep space, the moon and the bleak, terrifying Ogron planet, the Master emerges as being behind a Dalek-backed plot. The Doctor wins the day, but the Daleks escape him.

See *Doctor Who and the Space War*.

PLANET OF THE DALEKS (6 Episodes)
by Terry Nation

In pursuit of the Daleks, the Doctor lands the TARDIS on the planet Spiridon. He falls gravely ill, so Jo sets off for help. She meets old allies, the Thals, who are on a suicide mission to destroy the Daleks. Jo contracts a fungus disease and is cured by a friendly but invisible native. Survivors of a crashed Thal space vessel tell the recovered Doctor that there are thousands of Daleks on the planet, immobilised by cold. The Thals activate a bomb releasing an ice volcano, which in its turn re-freezes the Daleks for centuries.

See *Doctor Who and the Planet of the Daleks*.

THE GREEN DEATH (6 Episodes)
by Robert Sloman

The villagers of Llanfairfach in Wales are delighted when the local Global Chemicals firm gets a Government grant to build a full-scale refinery. But the project is fiercely opposed by ecologist Professor Clifford Jones. He has set up a commune in the valley and feels the refinery is a threat to his paradise—or 'Nuthutch', as the locals call it. A strange death in some disused mines brings UNIT to the scene. The Doctor discovers a swarm of giant green maggots and green slime—both fatal to touch—which have been caused by waste pumped from the refinery. The refinery's director refuses to discuss this with the Doctor. He has been taken over by Boss, the giant computer which has a will of its own and is obsessed with the success of Global—at any cost whatever. The Doctor successfully uses the blue crystal from Metebelis Three to counteract the powers of Boss. Jo Grant falls in love with the young professor, and leaves UNIT to marry him.

See *Doctor Who and the Green Death*.

1973/4
THE TIME WARRIOR (4 Episodes)
by Robert Holmes

Lynx, an alien space captain, lands his crippled starship in medieval times outside a castle belonging to the robber chief Irongron. Irongron offers shelter in exchange for modern weapons. Lynx uses his time machine to reach the 20th century to steal scientists and equipment to repair his starship. The Doctor, accompanied by a stowaway, journalist Sarah Jane Smith, uses tracking instruments to take the TARDIS to Irongron's castle ... and a struggle against medieval violence and alien science ends when Lynx's spaceship blows up.

INVASION OF THE DINOSAURS (6 Episodes)
by Malcolm Hulke

London is evacuated after prehistoric monsters begin suddenly appearing from nowhere. The Doctor and Sarah return to find London deserted and under martial law. At first they are arrested as looters, but once back with the Brigadier they discover an incredible plot to alter Time. A group of misguided idealists wants to reverse Time, wiping out all Earth's previous history, and returning it to a golden age before technological pollution. Captain Yates, the Brigadier's No. 2, has been converted to their cause and is working against UNIT. Thanks to his powers as a Time Lord, the Doctor is able to foil the scheme and keep Time on its proper course.

See *Doctor Who and the Dinosaur Invasion*.

DEATH TO THE DALEKS (4 Episodes)
by Terry Nation

A space plague attacks all creatures in the Galaxy. The antidote can only be found on the planet Exxilon, home of a now savagely hostile and degenerate race. The Exxilons have rejected all technology, since their perfect, automated City expelled them. The Doctor and Sarah find themselves caught up in a struggle between humans, Daleks and Exxilons for possession of the vital antidote. Helped by Bellal, a friendly native, the Doctor saves the precious antidote for humanity. One of the humans sacrifices his life to blow up the Dalek spaceship.

THE MONSTER OF PELADON (6 Episodes)
by Brian Hayles

The Doctor and Sarah return to Peladon (see 'The Curse of Peladon', 1972) where the spirit of the sacred monster Aggedor is spreading terror and death. The Doctor discovers that his old enemies the Ice Warriors, helped by a human traitor, are behind a plot to seize the mineral wealth of the planet.

PLANET OF THE SPIDERS (6 Episodes)
by Robert Sloman

The blue crystal the Doctor found on the planet Metebelis Three and gave to Jo Grant as a wedding present
(in 'The Green Death', 1973), is vitally important to
the giant Spiders who rule the planet. Using a group of
mystics at a Tibetan Meditation Centre as their
channel, the Spiders send an emissary to recover the
crystal. The Doctor and Sarah are transported to Metebelis, and the Doctor leads a revolt of the planet's human
slaves against their spider rulers. He defeats the Great
Queen of the Spiders, but in the process his body is
riddled with deadly radiation. The Doctor returns to
his friends on Earth, apparently a dying man. However,
the Tibetan Monk Cho-Je, in reality a Time Lord himself, accelerates the regeneration process. The Doctor
begins to change ...

See *Doctor Who and the Planet of the Spiders*.

1974/5
ROBOT (4 Episodes) by Terrance Dicks

The Doctor is in a coma, recovering from the effects of
his latest body-change. Meanwhile a mysterious *something* is breaking into top-secret government establish-
ments, stealing plans and parts for the new Disintegrator
Gun. The Doctor recovers in time to lead the investiga-
tion and a parallel inquiry by Sarah leads them to a
research establishment known as Thinktank. Here, a
group of dissident scientists, led by the formidable Miss
Winters, is planning to take over the world. To do this
they are using a giant Robot, designed by Professor
Kettlewell, who pretends to oppose them, but is really
on their side. Using Robot and Disintegrator Gun, the
Thinktank group steal a set of Destructor Codes. These

will enable them to start nuclear war by triggering off atomic missiles all over the world. They then issue a surrender ultimatum to the Government and retire to their fortified bunker, guarded by the Robot, and taking Sarah and Harry with them as hostages. In an attempt to destroy the Robot, the Brigadier shoots at it with the now-recovered Disintegrator Gun. Unfortunately the colossal infusion of energy this provides causes the Robot to grow to enormous size. Luckily the Doctor arrives in time with a solution of 'metal virus' brewed up in Kettlewell's laboratory. This first returns the Robot to its original size, then dissolves it into rust.

The world is saved, but Sarah cannot help regretting the necessary destruction of the Robot, for which she had developed a kind of affection. As consolation the Doctor offers her a trip in the TARDIS. At the last moment, Harry Sullivan insists on joining them ...

See *Doctor Who and the Giant Robot*.

ARK IN SPACE (4 Episodes)
by Robert Holmes

The TARDIS materialises on a fully-automated space station, which appears to be empty and deserted. In reality it contains the whole future population of Earth, stored away in deep-freeze until the planet is once more habitable. Due to a fault in the machinery they have failed to awaken on schedule. The Doctor discovers that the space station has been invaded by the Wirrn, giant alien insect-like creatures, who plan to destroy the humans and take over Earth. Together with Sarah and Harry, the Doctor defeats the Wirrn and repairs the space station so that the now-awakened inhabitants can prepare to return to Earth.

THE SONTARAN EXPERIMENT (2 Episodes)
by Bob Baker and Dave Martin

The Doctor, Harry and Sarah return to Earth by the space station's matter beam in order to rectify a fault in the transmat system. This will enable the rest of the 'Ark's' population to return to Earth. To the Doctor's horror he discovers that Styre, a Sontaran Officer, has reached Earth before him. The Sontarans are old adversaries of the Doctor. (See 'The Time Warrior', 1973/4). Field-Major Styre is conducting cruel experiments on human captives in order to discover the strength of human resistance to a planned invasion. The Doctor finally defeats him, making Earth safe for resettlement by the human race.

GENESIS OF THE DALEKS (6 Episodes)
by Terry Nation

The Time Lords send the Doctor, Harry and Sarah to the planet Skaro at a time when the war between Thals and Kaleds is reaching its final stage. The Doctor's mission is to prevent the birth of the dreaded Daleks who evolved out of this war. Hunted by both sides on a war-torn world, the Doctor eventually becomes the prisoner of Davros, the brilliant crippled Kaled scientist. Davros has invented a 'travel machine' to house the creature into which the Kaleds, genetically crippled by centuries of warfare, will eventually mutate. But Davros is obsessed by his own creation and is giving it destructive powers and a ruthless intelligence which were not part of the original design. These travel machines are destined to become the Daleks—an anagram of the name of the Kaled race. The Doctor helps to lead a revolt of Kaled scientists, themselves horrified by what Davros is doing. Davros, now totally obsessed, helps the

Thals to destroy his own people, changing sides in his determination to preserve the Daleks. Then he uses the Daleks, now fully operational first to wipe out the Thal City, then to destroy those remaining Kaleds who oppose him. The Doctor manages to entomb Davros in the fortified Bunker which has become his final refuge. Here the Daleks turn on Davros, destroying their creator. They set to work to prepare for the day when they will emerge to rule the Galaxy. The Doctor and his friends, their mission only partially successful, are whisked away from Skaro by a Time Ring ...

See *Doctor Who and the Genesis of the Daleks*.

REVENGE OF THE CYBERMEN (4 Episodes) by Gerry Davis

The Doctor, Sarah and Harry return to the space station only to find that they are in a completely different time-period. The space station is now fulfilling its original function as a space beacon, a kind of galactic lighthouse. Moreover, it is in the grip of a strange plague, which has reduced the crew to a mere handful. Learning that a mysterious asteroid appeared just before the plague began, the Doctor begins to suspect that the plague is not of natural origin. He discovers that the asteroid is the remains of Voga, the fabled planet of gold, and that his old enemies the Cybermen are planning to take over the space beacon as part of their plan to destroy Voga. The Doctor battles to save the space station and Voga, eventually defeating the Cybermen by the use of Vogan gold-dust, a substance which is deadly poison to them.

See *Doctor Who and the Revenge of the Cybermen*.

TERROR OF THE ZYGONS (4 Episodes)
by Robert Banks Stewart

Summoned back to Earth by the Brigadier, the Doctor investigates a series of mysterious attacks on North Sea oil rigs. Centre of the attacks is the village of Tulloch, very close to Loch Ness. The Doctor discovers that there *is* a monster in Loch Ness, the Skarasen, a creature half-animal, half-machine, created by the Zygons, an alien race whose crippled spaceship has rested on the bottom of the loch for hundreds of years. Unable to return home, the Zygons are now maturing their plans for the conquest of Earth. The Doctor defeats them and destroys their ship. The Skarasen, however, survives, to swim happily back to Loch Ness.

See *Doctor Who and the Loch Ness Monster*.

PLANET OF EVIL (4 Episodes)
by Louis Marks

Answering a Mayday call, intercepted while the TARDIS is in flight, the Doctor and Sarah arrive on Zeta Minor, a planet far out on the edge of the known universe. At a time far into the future a geological expedition has run into trouble; only its leader, Professor Sorenson, is still alive. A military party from Sorenson's home planet arrives to investigate. The Doctor and Sarah come under suspicion but when the whole party is attacked by anti-matter forces they are released. They leave the planet in the rescue rocket ship. Unhappily for them, however, part of the anti-matter monster is also aboard and begins to exact a hideous toll of the crew. The Doctor endures one of his most terrifying adventures before he is able to free the ship of this evil.

PYRAMIDS OF MARS (4 Episodes)
by Stephen Harris

The Doctor and Sarah are returning to the UNIT laboratory on Earth in the TARDIS. Suddenly the TARDIS is caught up by a mysterious force and thrown violently about. Sarah sees a face materialise which terrifies her. The TARDIS then makes the normal landing and the Doctor and Sarah find that they have arrived in the year 1911 and they are in an old Priory which existed on the spot before UNIT H.Q. was built. The house belongs to Marcus Scarman, an Egyptologist, who, during his explorations of Egyptian burial grounds, has stumbled upon an ancient feud between Horus and Sutekh from Osiris, and has unwittingly let loose terrifying forces upon the world. The Doctor manages to solve the mystery and prevent Sutekh from carrying out his plans to destroy the Universe.

See *Doctor Who and the Pyramids of Mars.*

THE ANDROID INVASION (4 Episodes)
by Terry Nation

The TARDIS lands near what appears to be a peaceful English village. But the inhabitants are strange and unfriendly, responding like robots to mysterious signals. The Doctor discovers that they are not on Earth at all, but in a replica village, built on their own planet by the Kraals, an alien race bent on conquest of Earth. The Doctor and Sarah return to Earth in time to foil the Kraal invasion. The Doctor reprogrammes an Android copy of himself, and uses it as a weapon against the Kraals.

THE BRAIN OF MORBIUS (4 Episodes)
by Robin Bland

The TARDIS lands on a bleak and storm-ridden planet, where Solon, a disreputable galactic surgeon, is carrying out strange experiments. The planet is also home of the Sisterhood, witch-like guardians of the mysterious Sacred Flame from which is prepared the Elixir of Life. The Doctor discovers that Solon is concealing the still-living Brain of Morbius, renegade Time Lord and cosmic villain supposed to have been executed for his many crimes. Solon is making a monstrous new body in which Morbius will live again to lead his followers in the conquest of the galaxy. The Doctor and Sarah have to battle with the Morbius Monster, revived and on the rampage, the suspicious Sisterhood, and Solon himself, who wants the Doctor's head for Morbius' new body, before Morbius is destroyed once and for all.

SEEDS OF DOOM (6 Episodes)
by Robert Banks Stewart

Deep in the permafrost of the Antarctic, scientists discover two vegetable pods. The Doctor identifies them as krynoids, an alien species of plant that is hostile to all animal life. One of the pods is destroyed, but the second is stolen by Harrison Chase, a rich and eccentric botanist. Back in England the Crinoid quickly develops into a sinister force threatening the entire western hemisphere, encouraging the native plants of Earth to turn against humanity. Many lives are lost before the Doctor and his allies in the World Ecology Bureau succeed in overcoming the menace.

THE MASQUE OF MANDRAGORA (4 Episodes)
by Louis Marks

The TARDIS is drawn off-course by the Mandragora Helix, an immensely powerful alien energy-complex. Unknown to the Doctor, an alien energy-form conceals itself inside the TARDIS, which subsequently lands back on Earth. The Doctor and Sarah find themselves in Fifteenth-Century Italy, in the province of San Martino. Here, the evil Count Frederico is planning to usurp the rule of his nephew, Giuliano. In this he is being aided by Hieronymous, the Court Astrologer, who is himself a secret member of a cult of star-worshippers.

The energy-form takes over Hieronymous, seeking to form a bridgehead so that the Mandragora Intelligence can rule the affairs of Earth through their chosen servants. The Doctor defeats the Helix by draining its energies, and the evil plans of Frederico and Hieronymous are foiled.

THE HAND OF FEAR (4 Episodes)
by Bob Baker and Dave Martin

Back on Twentieth-Century Earth, Sarah finds a fossilised hand. It is, in fact, the hand of Eldred, a Kastrian criminal executed by his own race. But Eldred's hand has the power to take over human victims, and with Sarah's unwilling help Eldred is regenerated in a nuclear research station. To save Earth from his powers, the Doctor is forced to take Eldred back to his own planet of Kastria. But in the hundred and fifty million year interval since Eldred's execution, Kastria's civilisation has ended. Eldred makes an attempt to regenerate his race, but fails. The Doctor and Sarah escape in the TARDIS and return to Earth, leaving Eldred to his solitary fate.

The Doctor receives a mysterious summons. He must leave for a vital mission on which Sarah cannot accompany him. The Doctor departs and Sarah is left on Earth.

11

Inside a Television Studio

In appearance a television studio is like a very big room (some are as big as a football pitch). In this huge empty space the sets are built, mainly all round the walls so as to leave a big space in the middle for the cameras to move about. A set might be a bedroom, or an office, or the inside of the TARDIS. Sets usually have only three walls. The cameras 'look' into the set through where the fourth wall should have been.

Usually four cameras are used in a production of *Doctor Who*. They are mounted on strong, heavy bases with small swivelling wheels underneath, and can glide about like Daleks. Each camera is linked by cable to a small television screen (or monitor) in the Director's control room. On these monitor screens the Director sees whatever the individual camera happens to be 'looking' at. Also in the control room there is a much larger screen called Output. By pressing buttons, the vision mixer can transfer any one of the four monitor pictures on to the Output screen: it is this picture which is recorded on to the videotape, and which you finally see on your television screen at home. These 'cuts', from one camera's view to another, are all worked out before the VTR (videotape recording) in the camera script. Planning these cuts is part of the Director's homework before the day of recording.

In a scene, say, between the Doctor and Sarah, the Director might use two of his cameras. Camera 1 is trained on the Doctor, camera 2 on Sarah. When the Doctor speaks, what camera 1 sees (the Doctor) goes on to the Output screen; when Sarah says a line, the vision mixer presses a button that brings in the picture from camera 2.

During that scene, cameras 3 and 4 are trained on the actors waiting in the next set to play the next scene. Let's say these are Harry and the Brigadier, and the set is UNIT Headquarters. They must wait poised as though in action, like two waxworks, until the Doctor and Sarah have finished their scene. Then the floor manager, who wears earphones and is in radio contact with the Director, will give a signal. This is Harry's and the Brigadier's cue to start acting. The pictures from cameras 3 and 4 will now be going on to Output. While Harry and the Brigadier are acting their scene, cameras 1 and 2 are gliding silently away from the first set to focus on whatever will be the following scene.

This is called 'continuous action', and once all television was produced like this, and was actually transmitted while the actors were acting (if an actor made a mistake, every viewer saw it). Now almost everything is pre-recorded, and many scenes are 'shot' two or three times until all is perfect.

For reasons of technical convenience scenes are sometimes recorded in segments, or out of story order—more like the way in which films are made.

At the end of the studio day, the Director has hundreds of feet of video tape (this is like tape-recorder tape only wider; it carries both sound and vision in electrical impulses). The Director can play this back to himself, and select the shots he wants to keep. This is called editing. Music and sound effects, such as explosions, can be added afterwards to the edited tape.

During a VTR a great many highly skilled people are at work. Everyone, both 'on the floor' (actors, cameramen, floor manager, etc.) and in the control room, is tense and anxious to see that his or her bit of the production is done to perfection. The Producer is there, of course, but at this stage more to advise than to supervise: he literally takes a back seat, but one from where he can see everything that is going on. However, the man of the moment during the VTR is the Director, and he sits at a vast bank of switches, buttons, microphones and flashing lights, facing the four monitor screens and the big Output screen. Also seated at this console, to either side of the Director, is his assistant (by microphone she tells the cameramen, who all wear earphones, which will be the next camera shot according to the script), the inlay operator (responsible for some special optical effects), the vision mixer (he makes the cuts), and the technical manager (in charge of the technical side of the whole studio). The control room is sometimes called the 'fish tank' because usually all the walls are glass, and from his place at the console the Director can see into two other smaller control rooms. One of these is for lighting, the other for sound. As the dramatic action moves from scene to scene, different sets have to be lit. The huge lights dangling from the studio roof were all put in position when the sets were built, but they are not switched on until needed. Electricity is expensive in such vast quantities, and anyway studios become uncomfortably hot. So the fewer unnecessary lights on the better. The people in the sound control room have banks of tape-recorders and turntables. The dramatic action may require them to bring in the sound of a motor car or a passing train, or the *Doctor Who* theme music.

If people are tense during a VTR, it's because there is plenty for them to worry about. A lot of things have to happen at once, and every one of them must happen *exactly* right. Some nights everything seems to go wrong. The actors play a perfect scene but a sound cue comes in fractionally early or late. A mysterious shadow, completely absent at rehearsal, appears to obscure the Doctor's face. A light or a camera breaks down, a sliding door refuses to slide. By the time all this has been sorted out the actors are naturally tired and edgy, and the performance 'drops'. One eye always on the clock (his recording time is strictly limited), the Director decides to take the scene again. Everything goes perfectly—until someone trips over a stool which falls with a clatter ...

Problems like these apply to any television recording, but *Doctor Who* has problems all its own.

No other show has so many special effects—monsters, spaceships, flashing instrument consoles, ray-guns. An experienced director once said flatly, '*Doctor Who* is the most technically complex show on British Television—and therefore, in the world!' Maybe this is stretching things a little, but it's not so very far from the truth.

A VTR recording night is in every sense of the word a climax. Writer, Producer and Script Editor may have started work on this episode as much as a year ago. The Director and his team, and all the production staff will have put in months of hard work. The actors will have been rehearsing for several weeks. But the success or failure of all their efforts will depend on what happens on the studio floor during the next few *hours*. What finally appears on the screen depends on what is recorded here and now. If the opportunity is missed or fluffed, it will never come again. Small wonder that there are tense nerves and crossed fingers in the studio as the countdown clock ticks down to the beginning of recording ...

12

4A—The Diary of a Production

Inside the *Doctor Who* Production Office each serial has a code number. This provides a convenient way to refer to serials not yet titled, or even written. The 'code' is simple enough. The first serial was A, the second B and so on. However, no one had allowed for the show's amazingly long life. As the years went by, the Doctor started on his way through the alphabet for a *second* time, Serials were coded AA, BB, CC etc. Then a *third* —AAA, BBB, CCC ... By the time the *fourth* trip through the alphabet was due to begin, everyone felt that AAAA, BBBB, CCCC, was going to be too much of a mouthful. So the code was changed. The next season's serials will be referred to as 4A, 4B, 4C etc....

4A is the first serial to come under the new coding. But this is by no means its only claim to special importance. It will be the first appearance of the fourth Doctor Who, Tom Baker, in the role which, hopefully, he will play for many years to come. It has to establish the character of the new Doctor, re-cap the change of body, and set him off on a new adventure exciting enough to make the viewers forget the change, and accept this new Doctor as the one and only ...

Terrance Dicks, now leaving the show after five years as Script Editor, is given the job of launching the new Doctor on his career. After all, he should understand the problems of writing for the show if anyone does. Next question—what shall the show be *about*? Bob Holmes, the new Script Editor, has already decided. He wants a story about a Robot ...

With this for his brief, the writer goes away to start work. Although he likes the idea of the Robot, he is acutely aware how much depends on its successful realisation in the studio. Next to the new Doctor, the robot will be his serial's 'main attraction'. It will have to be something really special. And what is it going to do? Just clank about smashing things?

The writer remembers a remark by a famous film critic, to the effect that in most monster films one ends up on the side of the monster. Like in King Kong—one of the earliest and best monster movies of all.

So—a *sympathetic* robot then, not so much evil in itself, as misguided, or misused, by some group of scientists in pursuit of their evil schemes. Sarah might even strike up a kind of sympathy with it ...

Once the writer begins thinking of the robot as a *character*, the story starts to take shape. Other characters emerge. The scientist who created the robot, well-intentioned but basically weak. The power-mad leader behind the whole scheme ... In these days of women's lib, it might be interesting to make her a woman. Then there would be Sarah, and the Brigadier. How would they come to terms with the Doctor's new incarnation? And what about the Doctor himself? What will he be *like* when he comes out of his coma?

All television writing goes in a series of steps, designed to ensure that what the writer envisages is also what the Producer and Script Editor need for the show. A kind of continuous collaboration and feedback takes place all the time, as more and more people become involved.

First step is the storyline. This is usually no more than a few pages, just a basic outline of the story. Once this is accepted, the writer is commissioned (which means paid) to write a story breakdown. This is a much more elaborate affair, a scene by scene breakdown of the entire serial. Its purpose is to show the way the writer intends to develop the story in more detail—and also that it is physically possible to reproduce the story on the screen. Here as always, the question of the show's budget, the amount of money the Producer can spend, is all-important.

Once the storyline is accepted, the writer is commissioned to write the four scripts, which are duly delivered some time later.

Even now the process isn't over. A writer's first scripts are called 'drafts'. They are read and discussed by the production team, and the writer will almost certainly be asked for some changes. These are known as the 're-writes'. After they are completed, the scripts are passed to the Director, the man who will be responsible for that particular show, who may ask for further rewrites of his own ... Television is very much a collaborative process.

In this case the first draft scripts are very close to what the production team wanted, and are passed straight to the Director.

Although he has comments on the story and the characters, most of the Director's worries are practical and technical. Are the resources of time and money at his disposal sufficient to put the show on the screen? Will the Robot be physically able to do all that is required of it? And what about that final sequence where the Robot grows to giant size—splendid stuff on the screen, but extremely difficult to realise in studio.

Production office and Director look at all these problems from slightly different angles. To use a military metaphor, the production team are the Staff Officers who look at their maps and work out their next objective, say the capture of a particular town. The Director is the soldier in the field who must take the men and equipment he is given and physically go out and do the job.

The Director of serial 4A is to be Christopher Barry, who is very experienced in the particular problems of *Doctor Who*. Some of his worries can be solved by the rewrites, which will reduce the number of exterior scenes. An extended sequence in which Sarah, in her car, is attacked by the Robot, is reluctantly dropped altogether.

Even with the projected cuts, the show is complicated and expensive. To cut still further will reduce the impact of the show ... At this point appropriately enough, modern technology came to the Doctor's aid. Exterior sequences on *Doctor Who* are usually filmed, interior sequences recorded on videotape in the studio. Filming is both slower and more expensive than videotape. But it looks more polished on the screen and, of course, enables the show to get out of doors, a vital element in an action serial.

However, it *is* possible to use videotape for exteriors. The BBC's Engineers have developed a sort of portable TV Studio, a lightweight mobile videotape unit, mainly designed to be used for outside broadcasts of sports events. But it *can* be used for drama. *Z Cars* have already videotaped such a show. There is another great benefit from this system. Trick shots, showing the Robot growing to enormous size, *have* to be done in studio, and then blended on to film. The slight difference in picture quality between videotape and film is sometimes detectable on screen. If this happens, the trick shots will look unconvincing. But with the whole show on videotape, the match between interiors, exteriors and special effects shots ought to be perfect.

The decision is taken. Serial 4A will be the first

Doctor Who entirely on videotape. There is one more problem. The lightweight videotape system is still less mobile than film itself. It works best if the action can be concentrated around one area. This means that all the exterior sequences need to be recorded on one location. And the script calls for roads, heathland, a cottage, a drill hall, UNIT H.Q. Someone remembers the BBC Engineering Training Department at Wood Norton, near Evesham in Worcestershire. This is a kind of small estate with various buildings and open areas, all fairly close together. Things begin to look more hopeful.

Working at top speed the writer completes his re-write within a matter of days, and the Rehearsal Scripts are duplicated. Sixty copies of each are needed, which gives some idea of the number of people concerned in a TV production. Now the production moves. The Director with his 'team'—assistant, secretary and assistant floor-manager—begin a seemingly endless series of meetings with all the many specialist departments who contribute to every TV show. In the middle of meetings with Design, Make-Up, Special Effects and Costume, the Director has to find time for casting. His team make endless phone calls to the BBC casting department, checking on the availability, and the price, of the actors he has in mind. One of the most important meetings is with Jim Acheson, who, as costume supervisor, is responsible for designing and building the Robot, which has to look not only massive and terrifying, but human and appealing as well! (Those who saw the show will remember how impressive was the finished result.)

After briefing meetings, there come follow-up meetings in which members of the various departments discuss their designs and plans with the Producer and Director.

Ideas are accepted or rejected, modified and amended.

Costumes are made, sets built in the BBC workshops. Gradually the production is taking shape.

Not all of these meetings are attended by the Producer and Script Editor. The attention of the Director and his team is rightly concentrated on just one show. But the production team has other things to worry about. There are *five* shows in the new *Doctor Who* season, and several of them are now in various stages of production. Other writers and directors are now beginning to demand their attention.

To change to a Naval metaphor, one ship is built, crewed and preparing for the launch—but there are four more ships in the fleet to be looked after. As the season as a whole gets under way, the attention of the production team will be divided and divided again. Producing a TV series is like a complicated juggling act in which someone is always tossing you an extra ball!

Towards the end of April, it is time to get serial 4A on the road—literally. The Director's team has prepared an 'OUTSIDE BROADCAST SCHEDULE', a twelve-page document containing everything anyone connected with the production needs to know. It gives departure and arrival times, hotels, a map, train times. It lists the plans for each day's recording, the precise location of each sequence, the artists, cameramen, props, technicians needed.

On the last Saturday in April a large number of people start moving towards Evesham. A huge scenery lorry sets off from the BBC TV Centre in Wood Lane. A minibus packed with Make-Up and Costume staff leaves from Main Reception. Actors and production staff converge on Evesham by train and car. Most important of all, the video unit with its mobile control room is on its way to Wood Norton.

Moving in and setting up takes up all Saturday and

Sunday morning. Early on Sunday afternoon, everyone is assembled and hard at work. TV production takes no account of anyone's plans for a leisurely weekend.

Then follow four days of very hard work. Scenes are set up, rehearsed, recorded. A move to a nearby location, then it's set up, rehearse, record again. Recording begins at nine and ends at seven. Allowing for an hour's preparation and an hour's tidying and clearing up, most people are working from eight to eight—a solid twelve-hour day. Evenings are spent discussing the day's work and planning the next. They work constantly against the clock, subject to minor technical malfunctions, and the unpredictable English spring weather.

The Director's assistant clutches a seemingly interminable list of shots, ticking them off one by one as they are completed. Slowly the list of ticked-off shots grows longer. By the end of the fourth day, the O.B. pre-recording is completed.

Weary but triumphant, the Director and his team return to London—but not, as you might expect, for a well-earned rest. *Doctor Who* serial 4A is now going into studio rehearsal.

A few days later, the Producer, Script Editor, Writer, Director and his team, and all the actors and actresses meet in a BBC rehearsal room for the 'read-through'. This takes place in a huge empty room, empty except for a long trestle table with chairs around it. Producer, Writer and Script Editor arrive, and stand chatting with the Director and his team. Actors begin drifting in, wearing casual rehearsal clothes, usually jeans and sweater. Everyone takes seats around the table. Coffee is served in BBC cardboard cups. The Director makes a little speech of welcome, and goes round the table introducing everyone by name—an impressive feat of memory.

The read-through starts. As the name implies, the actors simply read through the scripts of the serial, one after the other in story order. (This can be an unnerving ordeal for the writer. Few actors attempt any kind of performance on a read-through. Most just drone through the script in a kind of low mumble, saving their talents for later.)

As each scene is read, the Director's assistant times it with a stop watch.

The read-through of a four-part serial—which will take up nearly two hours of screen time—is a long and tiring business.

When it's over, the Director declares a brief coffee-break, and the actors wander off to the canteen. The Director, Producer, Script Editor and Writer go into a brief huddle. The assistant adds up her timings. The first episode runs a little short, the second and third seem about right, the fourth is a little long. At this stage no one worries too much, since read-through timings are necessarily approximate. Steadily more accurate timings will be recorded as the rehearsals progress. If any episode is particularly long or short, the news will reach the Script Editor well before the recording. He will then have to cut the script, which is usually simple, or lengthen it, which is invariably a problem.

At this point Producer, Script Editor and Writer leave. Producer and Script Editor return to their offices to work on the other serials now in production. (For the writer who is not a BBC employee but a self-employed freelance, this will be his last connection with the show for some time.) Further work on the script, usually for technical reasons, will be done by the Script Editor.

The writer goes home to start his next project knowing his script is in good hands. Later he will attend the studio recording.

The Director meanwhile is getting on with the job of rehearsing the first two episodes. These will be recorded on two successive studio nights. Scene by scene the scripts are rehearsed, discussed, rehearsed and rehearsed again. This goes on for the next two weeks. By the second week the actors are word-perfect, working without their scripts. The next stage in rehearsal is the 'Producer's run', held towards the end of the rehearsal period.

When the Producer and Script Editor return to the rehearsal rooms nearly two weeks later, the place is transformed. Coloured strips of tape mark out the areas of the sets which will be put up in the studio. A strange assortment of odds and ends has been scattered about. Old wooden chairs and tables and piles of tea-chests serve as control rooms and laboratories. Broomhandles take the place of UNIT rifles. Still in their everyday clothes, the actors run through the first two episodes. Despite the ramshackle props, everything is treated with deadly seriousness. This is their first public performance—even though it's before an audience of two.

After the run-through, another coffee break for the actors, another and longer discussion between Director, Producer and Script Editor. Episode one has 'spread' in rehearsal, and is now about the right length. Episode two, however, is now too long, and it seems likely that three and certainly four will be slightly over-length. The Script Editor promises to go through the scripts for possible cuts, holding them ready in case they are needed. The Producer feels that one actor, whose role has comic elements, is overplaying the comedy at the expense of the drama. The Director accepts the point, and promises to check the tendency in the few rehearsals remaining. He is very much aware that the Studio recording, the VTR, is almost upon him.

All too soon, the day arrives. Now for the first time the actors rehearse in the full technical complexity of the studio, with real sets, real props, wearing costume and make-up. Studio time is expensive; they are allowed this luxury for only one day. That same evening they will record the first episode.

You have read an account of what happens in a TV Studio in Chapter Eleven. As rehearsals start, the scene crew who have been working all night, are putting the finishing touches to the set. There is clattering and banging as some last-minute job is hurriedly finished. There follows a long, hard day under the hot studio lights. The actors go through their now-familiar moves, speak their now-familiar lines, but in a strange, hot, noisy, alien environment.

The technical crews rehearse *their* moves, ensuring that cameras, lights and sound-microphones are in the right place at the right time. The actors rehearse in continuous stops and starts, playing a scene, perhaps even part of a scene, over and over. They are asked for minute adjustments in position. 'Weight on the left foot, chin two inches higher for the close-up, move six inches further left when you come through the door, don't forget to step to the left when you get your cue.' All this in addition to remembering the lines, *and* keeping the 'sparkle' in their performance. Television is very tough on actors—and for that matter, on everyone else.

The rehearsal day comes to an end, there is a short break for supper and by just before 8 pm everyone is back in the studio. The atmosphere in the Director's control room is tense. The hands of the clock creep slowly towards the starting time. Over his microphone the Director calls, 'Good luck, studio.' The clock clicks round to 8 pm. The Director's assistant speaks into *her* microphone. 'Run telecine, opening titles. Go grams.'

The familiar swirling patterns fill the screen, the *Doctor Who* music pounds out, and the VTR has begun.

After two tense hours, the studio scenes of episode one are 'in the can'. Next day the whole gruelling process will be repeated with episode two. Then back to the rehearsal hall to start work on episodes three and four. These will be recorded in the same way two weeks later.

At last all four episodes are safely recorded. Even now the Director's work is by no means over. Next comes what many Directors feel to be the most creative part of their job—the editing.

No longer is the Director surrounded by hordes of people. By now he has safely in his possession miles and miles of videotape, sound and picture recordings which he can play backwards and forwards at will. Everything recorded at Wood Norton, everything recorded during all four studio nights. Now, alone and undistracted, he and his editor can link all these sequences, shot by shot, in the most dramatic and satisfying order. With most scenes he has a number of different takes to choose from. He can even link part of one take with part of another, taking the best from both. All these hours and hours of videotape will be steadily edited down, distilled to a precise 24 minutes 30 seconds per episode. Sound and music are added. (As well as Ron Grainer's famous theme music, played by the BBC's Radiophonic Workshop, the specially composed music written for a *Doctor Who* serial makes up a whole symphony in itself.)

Complete at last, serial 4A begins to face its audience. The first is small. Director, Producer and Script Editor watch a playback in the office of Bill Slater, Head of Serials, who takes a keen interest in Tom Baker's first performance as Doctor Who. His reaction is enthusiastic. All those who have worked on the show are much encouraged. But everyone knows that the final verdict rests with the viewers—and serial 4A will not be transmitted until the following January, still several months ahead.

The production team go back to their offices, to resume work on the Doctor's later adventures. The Director goes on to a completely different show, consoling himself that, whatever it is, it's sure to be easier than *Doctor Who*.

January comes round, and the show's first episode is transmitted. Public reaction is favourable, and viewing figures are good. 'Could be just curiosity,' someone argues. 'They're bound to want to see what he *looks* like . . .' But figures are good the next week and the week after that. Tom Baker is a success. 'Robot' is a success. *Doctor Who* is a success, just as it has been for so many years.

But there isn't much time for self-congratulation. As soon as he's polished off the Robot, the Doctor is due to tangle with the Sontarans. Then the Daleks, and the Cybermen. In fact, it's almost time to start worrying about *next* season . . .

NOTE: For the record, serial 4A was produced at a time of transition. Terrance Dicks had already 'handed over' the post of Script Editor to Robert Holmes, but Philip Hinchcliffe was still in process of taking over from Barry Letts. For the sake of simplicity the latter two are merged in the narrative, though in fact Barry Letts produced 'Robot' and Philip Hinchcliffe the subsequent serials.

The following pages show the same incident from 'Robot' in a number of different forms: storyline, story breakdown, script and Target novelisation.

Excerpt from Writer's storyline

Returning from their useless visit to Thinktank, the Doctor and Brigadier discuss the situation. The Doctor is convinced that Miss Winters is lying. The Robot has *not* been destroyed.

The Brigadier leaves for Whitehall. Alone in his laboratory, the Doctor gets a telephone call from an agitated Professor Kettlewell, who tells him the Robot has turned up at his cottage in a dangerously unstable condition. He begs the Doctor for help. The Doctor says he'll come at once.

He leaves a note for the Brigadier and hurries off.

Soon afterwards Sarah comes back to UNIT H.Q. to report on her visit to the SRS. She finds the Doctor's note and rushes off after him, fearing he has been led into a trap.

Benton tells her to wait for him, but she has already gone. Benton goes to round up a patrol.

Meanwhile the Doctor has reached Kettlewell's laboratory. It is dark, and apparently empty. The Doctor enters. As he looks round a giant form appears from the darkness. The Robot stalks menacingly towards him.

End of Episode Two.

Writer's story breakdown

18. Int. Doctor's Laboratory. Day.

The Doctor and Brigadier discuss the visit.
The Doctor says Miss Winters is lying. The Robot has not been destroyed.
The Brigadier leaves for Whitehall.
The Doctor is left alone, brooding. The telephone rings.

19. Int. Kettlewell's Laboratory. Day.

Kettlewell on the phone in a state of great agitation. He says the Robot has turned up in an unstable condition. Will the Doctor help? He will? Good! Kettlewell will be waiting at the cottage laboratory.

20. Int. Doctor's Laboratory. Day.

The Doctor puts down the phone, looks thoughtful. He scribbles a note for the Brigadier and leaves.

21. Ext. Road.

The Doctor drives along in Bessie.

22. Int. Doctor's Laboratory. Day.

Sarah comes back from SRS and reads the Doctor's note. Convinced the Doctor is walking into a trap, she rushes off after him. Benton prepares to follow.

23. Int. Kettlewell's Laboratory.

All is dark and silent. The Doctor enters, looks round. The Robot appears from the darkness and stalks menacingly towards him.

End of Episode Two.

(SARAH GIVES THE NOTE
TO BENTON)

SARAH: The idiot! He
thinks he can deal with
anything.

BENTON: We'd better
get after him. I'll round up
some of the blokes.

SARAH: Good idea. I'll
meet you there.

(BENTON OPENS HIS
MOUTH TO PROTEST,
BUT SARAH HAS GONE)

23. INT. KETTLEWELL'S
LABORATORY. DAY.

(THE SHUTTERS ARE UP,
THE ROOM IN SEMI-
DARKNESS.
THE DOOR OPENS, THE
DOCTOR ENTERS AND
LOOKS ROUND)

DOCTOR: (CALLING)
Professor Kettlewell! Are
you there, Professor?

(THE GIANT FORM OF
THE ROBOT APPEARS
FROM THE DARKNESS
AND STALKS

ROBOT: You are the Doctor?

DOCTOR: How do you do? I've been looking forward to meeting you for some time.

ROBOT: Please confirm your identity. You are the one known as the Doctor?

DOCTOR: Yes of course I am. And I'm very pleased to meet——

ROBOT: You are an enemy of the human race. You must be destroyed!

End of Episode Two.

Novelisation

Page 66 from *Doctor Who and the Giant Robot* by Terrance Dicks. Target Books.

Sarah threw down the note impatiently. 'The idiot! He thinks he can deal with anything.'

Benton said, 'We'd better get after him. I'll round up some of the blokes.'

'Good idea,' said Sarah. 'I'll meet you there!' She was out of the room before Benton could protest.

The Doctor drove up to Kettlewell's cottage in 'Bessie', his old Edwardian roadster. He jumped out of the little car and strode over to the door. To his surprise it was slightly ajar. Cautiously, he stepped into the darkened room and looked round. It took him a moment to accustom his eyes to the gloom, 'Professor Kettlewell,' he called. 'Are you there, Professor?'

An immense metal shape loomed out of the darkness, towering over even the Doctor's tall form. A booming voice said, 'YOU ARE THE DOCTOR?'

The Doctor peered up at the shadowy giant. 'How do you do? I've been looking forward to meeting you for some time.'

'PLEASE CONFIRM YOUR IDENTITY. YOU ARE THE ONE KNOWN AS THE DOCTOR?'

'Yes, of course I am. And I'm very pleased to meet——'

'YOU ARE AN ENEMY OF THE HUMAN RACE. YOU MUST BE DESTROYED.'

With amazing speed, the great metal hands lunged for the Doctor's throat.

13

How to Make a Monster
or
Blow up the World!

In nearly every *Doctor Who* adventure there is one moment everyone is waiting for. Up till then, you have only seen hints of the monster, a scaly foot or a mechanical hand. But now the moment has arrived! The monster is revealed. Here it comes, lurching from the shadows, eyes flashing, ray-gun blazing, advancing on to the brave Doctor and his terrified companions! However, what you don't see is the man from the BBC's Visual Effects department who is trailing behind the monster, turning off and on those flashing eyes. Nor do you see the perspiring actor who is staggering along inside the heavy costume of this terrifying alien invader from Space.

Most of the monsters and aliens in *Doctor Who* are really actors inside specially designed costumes. Usually the 'body' of the costume is built by the BBC's Costume department, while the head, claws, weapons and any other gadgets come from Visual Effects. Today, the Visual Effects department has a very large staff. There are many designers, each with a number of assistants. They have a large workshop, and even a mini-studio where working models can be filmed. But despite all the department's staff and equipment, the BBC produces so many television shows needing special effects that some of the work has to be done outside the BBC by specialist firms.

Jack Kine, Manager of Visual Effects, can remember

when things were very different: 'In the early days,' he says, 'there were just seven of us, in a temporary workshop, trying hard to keep up with all the productions requiring visual effects.'

The growth of the Visual Effects department and the ever-increasing complications of *Doctor Who* have gone hand in hand. As *Doctor Who* continued over the years, bigger and better effects were needed. The Producers wanted explosions, ray-guns, walls and doors that would melt, spaceships that would take off, and control-rooms to be blown up. Of course, Visual Effects also serves other shows. But by far the biggest 'customer' is *Doctor Who*.

Monster-making is often a combined operation between different departments at the BBC. Take, for instance, the Yeti. The bodies of these giant, shaggy snowmen were made by the Costume department, but the control unit that fitted into their chests was constructed by Visual Effects. In the case of the Ice Warriors, Visual Effects and Costumes combined to make the head and body, but the Make-up department then treated the area round the actor's mouth to match his face mask so that he was able to speak with his own voice (sometimes, as with the Daleks, the voice you hear is not that of the actor inside the monster costume). The clothes of the Autons came from the Costume department, but the plastic 'faceless' face, and the hinged hand that dropped away to reveal a ray-gun were from Visual Effects. You will also remember that when Autons fired at someone, the victim 'exploded'. This was the work of Visual Effects. A very small explosive charge was sewn into the victim's clothes, and this was detonated electrically at the right moment. In 'The Daemons', the stone gargoyle from the church that attacked the Doctor was the work of Visual Effects.

But apart from monsters, the Visual Effects department makes all sorts of other things. A space rocket is made with corrugated cardboard, silver paint, and dry-ice to provide the belching smoke for the take off. A frequently used material is pure latex which can be heated and poured into a plastic mould, then painted and processed to give various scaly and knobbly effects. Jack Kine and his assistants in the Visual Effects department pride themselves on being able to mould, crush, bash, twist or paint almost anything until it looks like something else. And, like everyone else in television, they have to worry about money. The skill of their jobs is to create exciting and interesting effects without spending a fortune.

There is nothing the men of the Visual Effects department like more than a really big explosion. At the end of 'The Daemons' the story required that the village church be blown up. For the filming, the director went on location and used a real village church. But for the final shot of the church, Jack Kine and his people made a beautiful model of that particular church. It was only seen on the screen for a moment before it suffered one of the biggest bangs Visual Effects had ever produced. All this was so well done, and the model church was so completely blown to pieces, that after the episode had been transmitted the then producer, Barry Letts, received an angry letter from a viewer. She had visited the village of the real church, and was more than a little annoyed that such a lovely church had been blown up just to make a TV programme!

If you want to know more about the strange make-believe world of special effects, you can read *The Technique of Special Effects in Television* written by

Bernard Wilkie, who is the BBC's Senior Visual Effects Designer. It is published by Focal Press, and costs £3.50, but you should be able to find it in your public library.

Next time you see a *Doctor Who* monster, give a thought to the actor inside, and a special thought to all the hardworking people who turned the writer's idea into what you actually see on the screen.

14

A New Life for the Doctor

What will be the Doctor's future—if one can really speak of the future for someone travelling through time?

At the time this book is being written, the Doctor seems to be loosening his connections with Earth, returning to his earlier role of the mysterious wanderer through the strange world of Space and Time. At the moment his fate is in the hands of Producer Philip Hinchcliffe, and Script Editor Robert Holmes. With two very successful seasons behind them, they are now well into production of their third. Philip Hinchcliffe feels confident that in the dangerous and disturbing world of today there is a real need for a show like *Doctor Who*. It provides an escape into fantastic alien worlds, where the monsters and horrors encountered are safely distanced by their settings. Today the appetite for fantasy and wonder, with the much needed release it offers, is greater than ever before.

Whatever happens to the Doctor on the screen we can now be sure that many of his adventures will be preserved for posterity, though in a rather different form.

As we said at the beginning of this book, television is an instant medium, hard to recapture once it has left the screen. Many of the Doctor's early television adventures are lost for ever. Enormous pressure on storage space forces the BBC to 'wipe the tapes' of a large proportion of its output. A certain number of *Doctor Who* shows have been preserved for the Television Archives, but many more are gone for good. Lost as TV shows, that is.

An ever increasing number are now being preserved in more permanent form as Target Books.

Through the Target novelisations you can relive adventures you have recently watched on your screen, or catch up with adventures that were shown before you were born. So far there are 27 Target books in print, and there are more in preparation. One way and another, it looks as if the Doctor will continue to entertain us for many more years to come.

GLOSSARY

Television Terms

Audition When a producer or director wants to see if an actor may be right for a part in a story, he asks him to act for him, perhaps in his office. Usually the actor just reads from the script, so that the Producer can hear what he sounds like. Sometimes more elaborate auditions are set up in which the actors will play scenes.

BBC British Broadcasting Corporation. It started in 1927 with radio (before that, from 1922, there was the British Broadcasting Company). BBC Television started in 1936, and was the first regular television service in the world.

Camera script Copies of this are given to the cameramen and some other technicians. It is the rehearsal script (see below) plus the Director's notes about how each scene is to be shot (also see below). This is the script in its final form.

Cut When the vision mixer changes the picture on the Output screen from that of one camera to another, that is a cut. (See 'Inside a Television Studio'.)

Close-up A very close shot of an actor, or an object on the set. A close-up usually means that the actor's face fills all the screen.

Cue A signal to tell an actor to start acting, to tell Sound Control to make sound, or to tell a cameraman to start shooting. It can be a spoken order, or even a nod of the head.

Director The man or woman who actually has to 'put

the show on the floor', meaning the studio floor. He 'directs' the actors and cameramen (see Diary of a Production on Page 74) in rehearsals, and during the recording.

Grams From gramophone, the old word for record-player. At the start of a VTR (see below) the production assistant tells Sound Control to 'Go grams'. This is their cue to play the *Doctor Who* theme music.

Inlay An inlay operator works in the Director's control room and is responsible for certain special effects on the television screen. For instance, there is a trick called colour separation overlay (CSO). You can have a person standing on a blue-coloured chair against a blue wall, and camera 1 is trained on them. Camera 2, meanwhile, is trained on a living-room set. By pressing the right buttons, the inlay operator can merge the pictures of camera 1 and 2, so that the pictures from the two cameras appear on one screen. If camera 1 has been fixed not to 'see' the colour blue (the chair and the wall), the effect will be of the actor standing in the living-room— in mid-air!

Producer He is as a general is to an army. He is in charge of directors, actors, technicians and everyone else. His is the final responsibility.

Ratings The number of people who watch a particular television show. Every week the BBC asks many thousands of people what shows they watched the previous week. From their answers it can be estimated how many millions of people probably watched each show.

Rehearsal Script The script without the Director's special notes for the camera shots. The actors learn their lines from the rehearsal script.

Script Editor Responsible to the Producer for all the

scripts. He works with the writers, reads what they send in. When a director wants a change in a script, the Script Editor either does it or asks the writer to do it.

Storyline What the writer firsts puts on paper. It gives a general idea of the story he has in mind, with few details.

Story-breakdown The next stage. This version gives the writer's ideas, scene-by-scene, of the script he wants to write.

Take A slang term, meaning a VTR (see below). It probably comes from 'taking' a photograph.

Telecine From 'tele' for television and 'cinematograph' (you get the word 'cinema' from that). In other words, a filmed sequence which is put on to the videotape (see below) in between the studio scenes. The short version of telecine is TK when talking, but sometimes TC when writing. (Some people think it would be much easier if everyone just called it 'film' since that's what it is.)

Titles The names that you see on the screen, such as *Doctor Who* and Tom Baker and the name of the director and so on, are all printed on cards which are 'looked' at by one of the cameras. The names, and the business of showing them on the screen, are called titles.

VTR This means videotape-recording, or the 'take'. A videotape-recording machine is like a huge tape recorder, but it records vision as well as sound so the magnetic signal is much more complicated and the tape has to be much wider than that for a sound-only tape.